T0166835

the

HIDDEN GARDEN

the

HIDDEN
GARDEN
MIR TAQI MIR

Gopi Chand Narang

*Translated from the Urdu
by* Surinder Deol

PENGUIN
VIKING
An imprint of Penguin Random House

VIKING

USA | Canada | UK | Ireland | Australia
New Zealand | India | South Africa | China

Viking is part of the Penguin Random House group of companies
whose addresses can be found at global.penguinrandomhouse.com

Published by Penguin Random House India Pvt. Ltd
7th Floor, Infinity Tower C, DLF Cyber City,
Gurgaon 122 002, Haryana, India

Penguin
Random House
India

First published in Urdu as *Usloobiyaat-e Meer* by Educational
Publishing House, Delhi 2013
This edition published in Viking by Penguin Random House India 2021

10 9 8 7 6 5 4 3 2 1

ISBN 9780670095001

Typeset in Minion Pro by Manipal Technologies Limited, Manipal
Printed at Replika Press Pvt. Ltd, India

www.penguin.co.in

MIX
Paper from
responsible sources
FSC® C016779

When bad times hit Mir, one of his admirers, an honourable citizen, arranged for a good house in a nice neighbourhood for him to live. At the back of the room there was a window that opened into a small garden. Many years passed. A friend came for a visit. He was surprised to find that the window was bolted shut. He asked the poet, 'There is a beautiful garden in the backyard. Why don't you open the window and get a natural view?' Mir directed the visitor's attention towards a pile of papers and said, 'I am so absorbed in taking care of this garden that I have no time for any other garden.' A long silence followed.

—Mohammad Husain Azad
Aab-e Hayaat

Contents

Preface

Chalo tuk Mir ko sun-ne k moti se pirota hai[1]

Mir Taqi Mir (1723–1810) was the first Urdu poet whose work engrossed and enthralled me. What a time I lived in and what amazing people I got to know! When I entered Delhi University in 1952 for my master's degree in Urdu, classes were held in the historic Dilli College, located in the vicinity of Ajmeri Gate. This is the same college where Mirza Ghalib was once offered a professorship. Its alumnus included Urdu's great writers and poets such as Imam Bakhsh Sehbai, Mohammad Husain Azad, Maulana Hali, Nazir Ahmed, Zaka Ullah, and many more.

Partition had created a great vacuum. This was not the Dilli everyone knew. Although new students were enrolling in different programmes, I was the only one in the Urdu postgraduate studies. Everything had changed. There was a

---

[1] *n rakho kaan nazm-e shaa'iraan-e haal par itne / chalo tuk Mir ko sun-ne k moti se pirota hai* (Don't pay too much attention / to poets of the day. / Let us go and listen to Mir. /He does not use words. / He beads pearls in his poetry.)

time before Partition when Baba-e Urdu Maulvi Abdul Haq used to come here to teach Wajhi's *Sabras*, a Dakani prose masterpiece. In the riots preceding it, the office of Anjuman Tarraqqi Urdu in Daryaganj, where the esteemed Maulvi was secretary, had been reduced to ashes. Some half-burnt Urdu books of the Anjuman were available on the pavements of the nearby Urdu Bazar, which I bought. Ibadat Barelvi, who was popular among the progressives, had also left Dilli and gone to Lahore, where he had joined Oriental College. Among the old hands, only Khwaja Ahmed Faruqi was still there, and he lived in a little shack next to the historic Ghaziuddin madrasa adjoining the college building.

Interestingly for me, Khwaja Sahib was writing a book on Mir. During those days, Urdu text was handwritten for printing, and he assigned me the responsibility of proofreading the calligraphed text on chemically treated yellow sheets. Gradually, Mir's couplets found a place in my heart, and my moments of solitude, I heard echoes of Mir's lyrical voice. For a young student in his twenties, this was a riveting experience. It was also a time when I had an opportunity to read Mir's autobiography, *Zikr-e Mir*. Another work that greatly influenced me was Mohammad Husain Azad's *Aab-e Hayaat*. Azad painted a picture of Mir's life that was magical and full of colourful episodes and vignettes that left a strong imprint on the reader's mind.

Mir has been called *Khuda-e Sukhan* (the God of Poesy). It is not known who used this title for the first time, but it finds a prominent place in the history of Urdu literature. Azad emphasized the simplicity and flow of Mir's poetic style and this comment too gained traction. Among the great Urdu poets like Nasikh and Ghalib, there was a consensus that Mir was like a pathfinder and a great master poet. Who is not familiar with Ghalib's tribute:

Ghalib apna y aqiida hai baqaul-e Nasikh
aap be-behra hai jo mo'taqid-e Mir nahien

Ghalib, it is my firm belief, also supported by Nasikh,
you are not worthy of letters,
if you do not believe in the greatness of Mir.

Mir received unconditional praise from many others too. When the appreciation is so wholehearted and unqualified, it is often considered futile to go any deeper. There was no such thing as literary criticism at that time, except a comment or two in *tazkiraha*s (chronicles of poets). The point regarding 'simplicity and flow' attained the status of a mantra. However, there was another track that got people's attention: 'When he goes high, Mir really touches great heights, but when he comes down, he goes straight into the ground.' Mir was thus presented as a poet of seventy-two *nishtar*s (lancets)— great couplets that straightaway enter one's heart—while the rest was all low-quality crap. Surprisingly, when a couplet of Mir was quoted from thousands of his verses to make a point, people said this was a nishtar. There was, however, no definition of which couplet was a lancet and which was not. When this discussion got nowhere, scholars like Maulvi Abdul Haq (who compiled and published the first *Intikhaab-e Mir* at Anjuman), Nawab Jafar Ali Khan Asar Lakhnavi, Waheeduddin Saleem, and Dr Syed Abdullah got back to their comfort zone of labelling Mir as a poet of simplicity and flow.

This was not an unfair description, but Mir was a love poet of great magnificence. His verse contained magical features that no one discussed. Mir's life story is also filled with terrible hardships, pain, and suffering. He had an unfulfilled love affair followed by a bout of madness early in his youth. No one tried to unravel what accounted for the torment of his unconscious and his unusual self-esteem and extraordinary disdain for others.

In the environment of total despair and despondency that gripped the subcontinent in the aftermath of the partition, the rediscovery and revival of Mir were inevitable. Firaq Gorakhpuri (1896–1982) was the first to tread this path. He was fascinated by Mir's Hindi roots and the rasa of his Sanskrit poetics. Around the same time, across the border, Nasir Kazmi (1925–72) led Mir's widespread revival. He compiled an *Intikhaab*[2] of Mir's verse with a stimulating introduction. Pak Tea House, situated on the Mall Road in Lahore, was the hub of all avant-garde literary activity. Two discussions with Nasir Kazmi at Pak Tea House, which were initiated by Intizar Husain, are now part of Kazmi's *Intikhaab*. They were first published in *Savera*, an influential literary journal. The time to study Mir more seriously had finally arrived. In his perceptive and insightful commentary, Kazmi cast a wide net, discussing not only both Ghalib and Iqbal in the context of Mir, but also considering the post-Partition mood—the feelings of sadness and vagrancy, and an atmosphere of despondency and

---

[2]   Nasir Kazmi, *Intikhaab-e Mir* (Lahore: Jahangir Book Depot, 2001)

suffering on both sides of the border. Kazmi, a cult figure and a leading poet of modernism, proved to be a trendsetter, and his poetry echoed Mir's intriguing personality, forlorn sadness, and unusual alienation.

This was also the time when a revolution was sweeping the world of literature and philosophy following the posthumous English publication of Swiss linguist and semiotician Ferdinand de Saussure's (1857–1913) path-breaking linguistic theories. After completing my doctorate at Delhi University, I had an opportunity to learn and absorb these new ideas in humanities during my tenure at the University of Wisconsin, Madison. What surprised me most was the great affinity between these new discoveries and some of the ancient Indian poetics' thought processes. The DNA, which is of great value in the personal identification process, can also unfold, metaphorically speaking, hereditary secrets in the structural investigation of literary thought and unravel concealed facts about a poet that were not previously known or examined. After returning to India, and especially during my tenure at Jamia Millia Islamia, I got into literary criticism as a field of research and study. At Jamia, I started organizing yearly literary seminars on shared Indo-Pak themes.

During that time, I got an invitation from the Karachi Anjuman Tarraqqi-e Urdu to deliver the Maulvi Abdul Haq Memorial Lecture on Mir's poetry. Since the subject was close to my heart, I wanted to talk about aspects of Mir's oeuvre which no one had touched upon, and which needed in-depth attention. The first draft of my presentation was received well and the Karachi Anjuman published it in 1981. I continued to add to this work, and the completed book-long manuscript, titled *Usloobiyaat-e Meer*, was published from Delhi in 1984.

Mir's contemporaries included some prominent names. Everyone recognized Mir's mastery over lustrous poetic language, his breadth and depth of inventive meanings, and the superb lyrical quality of his verse. Still, for most of the eighteenth and the nineteenth centuries, the opinion about his standing as a poet was limited to a few attributes of flow and simplicity. What constituted Mir's creative signatures and how to identify the roots of his work and the directions they led were not looked into deeply enough. In that sense, this book is the first of its kind and fruition of that endeavour. Mir's work's serious critical look must go beyond traditional theses of simplicity and flow and a synthesis of Persian segments with Prakritik Rekhta (the vernacular dialects that existed alongside Sanskrit and the early prototype of Urdu).

Mir's greatness as a poet does not depend on one or two factors. He said it beautifully in his self-assessment: *Rekhta rutbe ko pahunchaaya hua us ka hai* (Rekhta reached the pinnacle of its glory because of his efforts). How did he do it? It resulted from a number of factors, including the mixing of magical formulations and the creative use of language that touched the reader's heart. What are the identifiable elements and the deep-seated markers of these attributes? I have been trying to unravel these hidden aspects. It has not been a smooth ride. Mir hinted about his Dakani *maa'shuuq* (beloved), *maa'shuuq jo apna tha baashinda dakan ka tha,* i.e., the colourful raw Dakani of south India. He also said that if there were rawness and wrinkles, he straightened and perfected it with his extraordinary creative skills as an artist.

Rekhta was an evolving and imperfect medium at that time. Mir turned it into a gemlike literary and gushing language of ghazal—highly aesthetic, skilful and rich with inventive meanings. Ghalib was deeply under Bedil's influence, but it is also correct to say that the vessel he needed to fashion the preciousness of his verse, the ingenuity of thought, and innovative subjects also came from Mir. Urdu had to become 'Urdu' before it became *Urdu-e Mualla* of Ghalib. Mir forged Urdu in the inner fire of his creativity. All the pathways of ghazal in the nineteenth century and later find their source in Mir. To call Mir a poet of simple conversational style is not doing justice to him, although he wrote much of his poetry in the people's language.

It is impossible to know about the tragic mass suffering caused by 1857 without going through Ghalib's letters. In the same way, we cannot appreciate the magnitude of the pillage, loot, and ruination during the invasions of Nadir Shah (1739) and the repeated plunder of Ahmad Shah Abdali (from 1747 onwards), and also the infighting between the Jats, Marathas, Rohillas and others without going into the soul of Mir's verse and his life. Mir's story is not just his own story; it is a testament to the miseries suffered by Delhi as a city and its residents. It is a story of the river of fire he had to wade through to survive in those times: *ujre nagar mein jaise jale hai charagh ek* (in a pillaged town engulfed in darkness shines a distant, tiny lamp somewhere). This was the same glittering city Mir had earlier eulogized and loved thus:

Dilli ke n the kuche auraaq e musavvar the
jo shakl nazar aai tasviir nazar aai

The lanes of Dilli were not lanes.
They were more like pages from an album.
Every face that you saw was like
a magnificent heart-stopping image.

No one could guess better than Ghalib what the heartbroken
Mir must have gone through when he shaped and perfected
Rekhta in those challenging times marked by violence,
barbarianism, and a complete breakdown of law and order.

rekhte ke tumhien ustaad nahien ho Ghalib
kahte hain agle zamaane mein koi Mir bhi tha

You're not the sole virtuoso of the craft of Rekhta, Ghalib!
People say that in the times gone by, there was a poet called Mir!

Mir is a poet of the fire of love and torment that impacts us
slowly. He is a poet of agony and suffering, as well as courage
and audacity. Before embarking on his poetry, it is important
to understand Mir's life's key events so that the reader
becomes familiar with the roots of Mir's pain and scars of his
psyche. He is like a candle that burns and melts continuously.
Mir is not only a poet of unrequited love; his voice reveals
and recreates echoes of the medieval age's soul-touching
transcendental thought of the bhakti tradition and spirituality
that runs parallel to the self-consuming mystic narrative of
Mansur and Majnun.

   Mir is not a simple poet by any means. This book attempts
to uncover multiple aspects of Mir's creativity. I have tried
to unwrap every hidden pathway, every dark trail that

zigzags, every footprint that shows something new, and every trajectory leads to a more hopeful future. There is a reason why almost after three hundred years, Nasir Kazmi said, 'The night of Mir's age has joined the dark night of our age.' The creative agony of Mir's verse reverberates the epoch of untruth that we live in. A poet's greatness lies in the fact that the poetic voice echoes trials and tribulations of ages that follow.

To mould the bewitching verse of Mir and its hidden delights into a modern Western language is not an easy task. For this creative endeavour, I wholeheartedly thank Surinder Deol, who has been my translator and associate for several years. Working together, we have covered a lot of ground. The Urdu text of the ghazals in the book has been drawn from *Kulliyaat-e Mir*, Vol. 1 published by the National Council for Promotion of Urdu Language.

Books have been written about Mir, and more will be written in the future, but this book attempts to open a new vista that has never been tried before. I hope that this English rendition of Mir will pave the way for further appreciation of his multidimensional work—a new critical discourse on Khuda-e Sukhan Mir, the first master poet of Urdu.

Gopi Chand Narang
New Delhi
December 2020

The Life of Mir Taqi Mir

The Agony and the Ecstasy

Mir was born in February 1723 in Akbarabad (as Agra was known then). He was named Mir Muhammad Taqi. When he grew up, he chose Mir as his *takhallus* (nom de plume). His ancestors had migrated to India from Hijaz in Iran a few generations ago. They first came to Dakan, then moved to Ahmedabad, and finally settled in Agra. His grandfather got the job of a *faujdaar* (a position in the Mughal army) and he lived a decent life; he died while he was travelling to Gwalior, leaving behind two sons. Mir's father, a dervish who was called Ali Muttaqi out of reverence, pursued the path of inner knowledge from his early age. Over the years, he gained a lot of followers within and outside the community. He remained busy day and night, his eyes moist with tears, in the remembrance of God. He was a man of utmost humility, a man free of prejudice, a perfect Sufi. He never became a burden for anyone else. In his autobiography, *Zikr-e Mir*, Mir talks about his father in a highly respectful and reverent tone, dwelling at length about the lessons that his father gave him from his early years. Here, in a nutshell are some of the things he was told:

> *ai pisar i'shq bavarz, I'shq ast k dariin karkhaana mutasarrif ast:* Son, always adopt love because love is the dynamic force that binds and controls this universe. Nothing great can happen unless you put a lot of love into your endeavour. If you take love out of your life, it becomes barren. All things around you are the manifestation of love. Water is love, so is fire. Even death is love's drunken stage. The night is the time when love sleeps; the day is when it wakes up. When you fill your heart with love, it attains perfection. Virtue is its union with love; sin arises when it separates itself from love. Paradise is attractive because it is filled with love; hell is a place of horror because there is no love to be found there. The practice of love is more significant than any prayer or pursuit of knowledge.
>
> Son, this world is nothing but a momentary excitement. Don't indulge too much in it. Love for God is the only real thing. Prepare for the journey that starts after this life is over.
>
> My son, you are the treasure of my life. What kind of fire burns in your heart? What is your passion? What do you want to be in your life? (When Mir heard his father ask these questions, he had no answer; tears rolled down his cheeks.)
>
> Son, be a nightingale whose spring never ends. Admire beauty whose colours never fade. Keep your heart always strong. Always be ready to face odds in life. The world

changes continuously. Do not be depressed when things get bad.[1]

There is no doubt that these teachings had a lasting impact on Mir's psyche, and he tried to live his life following these high ideals. Mir mentions that one day his father felt the urge to go to Lahore to meet another Sufi who gave sermons by the river Ravi. The old man reached Lahore with great difficulty, but to his disappointment, this so-called Sufi was a fraud who was deceiving poor people by muttering some words in Dari language which they did not understand. On his return journey, God rewarded his father by giving him a disciple, known as Sayyid, whom he brought with him to Agra, and this guest gradually became a member of the household. Sayyid taught Mir, who was seven years old at the time, to read the Quran. Mir called this person 'uncle' out of affection. His father and his 'uncle' became spiritual companions, and they could not live without each other's company. When Sayyid died, a part of his father died with him. Mir wrote, 'My father threw away his turban, tore open his shirt, and scarred his chest with constant battering.' On the third day after the death, when friends and admirers gathered to mourn, Mir's father announced that from that day onwards, he should be called Aziz Murda—someone who has lost a dear friend or a companion. He became famous by this name, and he spent the rest of his life shedding tears each day.

---

[1] Nisar Ahmed Faruqi, *Zikr-e Mir*, Urdu ed. (Delhi: Maktaba Burhan, 1957), pp. 25–98. Sharif Husain Qasmi, *Zikr-e Mir*, Persian ed. (New Delhi: Qaumi Council Bara-e Farogh-e Urdu Zaban, 2011).

Before he died, Mir's father sent for Mir and his stepbrother, Hafiz Muhammad Hasan, who was not very friendly towards Mir. The father gave Hafiz three hundred books telling him that as a fakir he had no other possession. But then he turned his face towards Mir and told him, 'Son, I owe three hundred rupees to the people in the market. You have to pay this debt.' Mir asked him, 'How will I do that? I have no money.' His father replied, 'Do not worry. God will take care.' A messenger came a few hours later carrying five hundred rupees from one of Sayyid's disciples. The debt was paid, and the remaining funds were used by Mir to give his father a decent funeral.

Putting his younger brother, Muhammad Razi, in charge of the family, Mir made his first trip to Delhi and luckily received an allowance of one rupee a day from a nawab who was one of his father's admirers. But that arrangement did not last long because Nadir Shah invaded and pillaged Delhi in 1739. Thousands were killed in the course of one night. In the morning, Nadir's warrior chief appeared and read a verse that all men in Delhi worth killing had been killed. This carnage changed the fate of almost all nawabs and nobles overnight. Mir went to Agra, but he was disappointed to find that the people who had professed care for his father and the family turned away. Mir was left with no option but to return to Delhi.

It was on this trip that he sought refuge in the home of Sirajuddin Ali Khane Arzu, a learned scholar of Dilli who was highly respected by writers of the time. Khane Arzu was the maternal uncle of his stepbrother Hafiz. Initially, he was friendly towards Mir, but after receiving a letter from Hafiz, his attitude changed overnight. The letter advised Khane Arzu to treat Mir 'like a snake in the grass; do not show him any courtesy; in fact, it would be good to have him killed'. Khane Arzu did many things to harm Mir. He wrote in *Zikr-e Mir*, 'If I am asked to write about Khane Arzu's enmity in detail, it would require a separate volume.' But what was Mir hiding? What did his stepbrother write privately, which turned Khane Arzu against Mir overnight? Why did he have to leave his house? What Mir concealed in *Zikr-e Mir*, he revealed in two short *masnavi*s (poems), after he had moved to the safety of Lucknow, which is quite revealing.

It was around that time that Mir started to have a very strange experience. From his early childhood, Mir was in the habit of looking at the moon at night when he was alone—a habit reinforced by one of his mother-like caretakers. Following his rift with Khane Arzu, Mir moved to a small room where he lived alone. At night, when he looked at the moon, he began to perceive a lovely feminine figure inside it. With time, the figure became lovelier; it appeared more like a fairy or a houri than an ordinary human being. Mir developed symptoms of madness. People felt unsafe in his company. This madness reached a point when people around him started to think about placing him in confinement, chained, and left alone to die. The wife of one of his father's disciples saw the miserable condition in which Mir lived. Out of compassion, she spent a great deal of money on his treatment. He took a few months to recover. The madness vanished, his ravings stopped, his brain gradually started to work again, he was able to sleep, and once again, he started to write poetry.

Why did this madness start? What was the trigger? Two of Mir's masnavis provide hints that while Mir was about eighteen years old, he fell in love with a girl. She was married, but because she was part of the family, she did not observe purdah from him. This love affair caused a great deal of suffering to both lovers. Mir did not talk about it in his book *Zikr-e Mir* or to anyone. Repressing it ripped his heart apart, and he carried with him all his life the wound of unrequited love and whatever psychological effect the madness left behind. We see the imprint of this tragic affair in all his poetic work.

A close reading of the masnavis *Muaamlaat-e I'shq* and *Khwab o Khayaal* reveals that the speaking voice is none other than that of the poet himself. Mir has provided sufficient poetic account of what happened in his early years and why he had to leave his parental home in Agra. The first masnavi appears to be about a casual affair—more like a love play—with someone who was a frequent visitor to the household or a guest of the family, which ended in separation. The second masnavi is more about a poignant engagement where the lover shows great affliction and deep wounds after the affair ended. Presumably, the person of Mir's love interest was closely related to his unfriendly stepbrother. In this masnavi, Mir soulfully articulates how after receiving one shock after another, he developed a severe psychic disorder, something akin to what is described as *junuun* (unbounded madness in the pursuit of love of the beloved).

In *Muaamlaat-e I'shq*, Mir says:

ek sahib se ji laga mera
us ke a'shvon ne dil thaga mera

ibtida mein to y rahi sohbat
naam se un ke thi mujhe ulfat
khuubi un ki jo sab kaha karte
gosh mere udhar raha karte
bakht-e bargashta phir jo yaar hue
ik tarah mujh se ve do-chaar hue
kya kahuun tarz dekhne ki aah
dil jigar se guzar gayi vo nigaah

ek muddat talak y sohbat thi
kabhu ulfat kabhu y kulfat thi
rafta rafta suluuk biich aaya
haat paaon ko apne lagvaaya
gaah be-gaah paaon phailaate
meri aankhon se talve malvaate
chal kar aate the jab kabhi iidhar
paaon rakhte the meri aankhon par
dekhne mein to paae-maali thi
husn se chaal y n khaali thi
hans ke seene p paaon rakh dete
dil mera yuun bhi haath mein lete
kya kahuun kaisa qad-e baala hai
qaalib aarzu mein dhaala hai

ek din farsh par tha mera haath
baatein karte the ve bhi mere saath
paaon se ek ungli mal daali
lutf se dard vo n tha khaali
dard se ki main ne betaabi
dast-e naazuk se der tak daabi

yaad aate hain aise lutf jo ab
guzre hain jaan-e gham-zadah p ghazab

baare kuchh barh gaya hamaara rabt
ho saka phir n do taraf se zabt
vaaste jis ke tha main aavaara
haath aaii mere vo mah-paara
chand roz is tarah rahi sohbat
pyaar ikhlaas raabta ulfat
ho gaaye bakht apne bargashta
phir kiya aasmaan ne sargashta
baat aisi hi ittefaaq pari
k hui sar p furqat aan khari
lagi kahne k maslahat hai y
kitne rozon juda tu mujh se rah
yuun bhi aata hai i'shq mein darpesh
k nishaan-e bala hon ulfat kesh
main uthaaya nahien hai tujh se haath
kurhiyo mat tu hai meri jaan ke saath
is judaaii ka mujh ko bhi gham hai
kya karuun aarzu muqaddam hai
main kahuun kya mujhe n apna hosh
jaise tasviir saamne khaamosh
un se rukhsat hua jo baa'd-e shaam
tiirah dekha jahaan ko har gaam
yuun hua un ke kuuche se aana
jaise hove jahaan se jaana
ab jo ghar mein huun to afsurda sa
chaarpaaii p huun to murda sa
haal dil ka kahuun jo hamdam ho

karuun paighaam kuchh jo mahram ho
ji mein kuchh aaya ro ke beth raha
dil zada chapka ho ke beth raha
yaad kar rouun un ki kaun si baat
kis tarah kaatuun hijr ke auqaat
muddat-e hjir agar tamaam hui
varna apni to sub-h shaam hui[2]

I fell in love with someone irresistible.
Her coquetry robbed me of my heart.
In the beginning, my association
rested on the love of her name.
Everyone praised her, so fond of her.
I furtively listened to such talk.
Luckily, we became good friends.
This is how we came very close.
How can I describe the way she talked?
Her gaze pierced my heart!

Our association continued for some time.
Sometimes it was love, sometimes vexation.
Slowly, how we behaved became an issue.
I was permitted to touch her hands and feet.
Sometimes, she extended her feet.
She used my eyes to touch her feet.
When she would come to my side,
she placed her feet on my eyes.

---

2   Mir Taqi Mir, *Kulliyaat-e Mir,* vol. 2 (New Delhi: National Council for Promotion of Urdu Language, 2007), pp. 210–19.

We were stepping into ruination.
But there was a pleasure in all this.
Smilingly, she would place her foot on my chest.
She played with my heart.
What can I say about her tall swaying self?
A body moulded by desire!

One day, my hand was on the floor
while she spoke of love with me.
She used her foot to stroke one of my fingers.
That pain was mixed with great pleasure.
With her delicate hand, she kneaded it for long.
When I remember these little delights
terrible things happen to my saddened heart.

Slowly, we got more intimate.
There was a loss of control on both sides.
Something that I was madly in search of
I found that moon-faced beauty, fortunately.
Days passed like this with her.
Love, openness, contact, affection—
suddenly, our luck took a turn for the worse.
The heavens turned our good fortune.
Something surfaced, and we were
struck by the calamity of separation.
She said we need to be prudent.
You have to stay apart for some days.
It happens in love.
You have to get rid of all signs of love.
Though I do not want to leave you.

Do not feel sad; you're the confidant of my soul.
I will suffer in separation too.
What to do when desire faces an obstruction?
What can I say? I had no control over my senses.
Like facing a picture that has no voice.
The evening I took leave of her,
I saw nothing but darkness in front of me.
I turned from her company
as if I had left my world behind.
I find myself in my house depressed;
I lay lifeless on my bed like a corpse.
I could share the malady of my heart if I had a friend.
I could have a conversation if I had a confidant.
When I remember something, tears come to my eyes.
Heart-broken, I sit silently, dumbstruck.
Of all the charming things about her,
which one should I talk about?
How should I spend these moments of separation?
If I meet her, my suffering might diminish.
I can come back and be counted among the living.
My life was filled with parting from the sweetheart.
Mornings came, and the evenings went by!

In his second masnavi, *Khwab o Khayaal*,[3] Mir describes his traumatic departure from his hometown. The affliction became more severe, and the pain unfathomable. It appears from the nature of the text that it was a serious involvement, a heart-wrenching encounter, and as a result, Mir was forced

---

[3]   Ibid., pp. 239–44.

to leave Agra. Mir talks of the agony of leaving home against his wishes and how miserable he felt. He also reveals what he had concealed in *Zikr-e Mir*—that this tragic love relationship was the reason for his obsession: the lovely face he saw in the moon and his strange fixation with that image. This masnavi touchingly narrates the details of Mir's ailment and the treatments on the way to recovery.

chala akbarabaad se jis ghari
dar o baam par chashm-e hasrat pari
k tark-e vatan pehle kyonkar karuun
magar har qadam dil ko patthar karuun
dil e muztarib ashk e hasrat hua
jigar rukhstaane mein rukhsat hua
jigar jor e gardon se khuun ho gaya
mujhe rukte rukte junuun ho gaya

nazar raat ko chaand par gar pari
to goya k bijli si dil par pari
nazar aaii ik shakl mahtaab mein
kami aaii jis se khur o khwaab mein
use dekhon jiidhar karuun main nigah
vohi ek suurat hazaaron jagah
saraapa mein jis ja nazar kijiye
vahien u'mr apni basar kijiye

jo dekhuun to aankhon se lahu bahe
n dekhuun to ji par qayaamat rahe
kahien naqsh e diivaar dekha use
kahien garm raftaar dekha use

kabhu suurat dilkash apni dikhaaye
kabhu apne baalon mein munh ko chhupaaye
gale mein mere haath daale kabhu
tarah dushmani ki nikaale kabhu
har ik raat chande y suurat rahi
isi shakl-e vahmi se sohbat rahi

tabibon ko aakhir dikhaaya mujhe
n piina jo kuchh tha pilaaya mujhe
daron khud bakhud be-havaasi rahi
pareshaan dili aur udaasi rahi
kiya band kothari mein mujhe
k aatish junuun ki magar vaan bujhe
n aave koi dar se mere kane
k kya jaaniye kaisi sohbat bane

ghalat kaari-e vahm kuchh kam hui
vo sohbat jo rahti thi barham hui
vo suurat ka vahm aur divaangi
lagi karne darpardah begaangi
n dekhe meri or us pyaar se
gharibaana sar maare diivaar se
kahien tuk tassalli kahien be-qaraar
kahien shauq se mere be-ikhtiyaar
kahien dil apna dikhaave mujhe
meri befaaii jataave mujhe
n aaii kabhu phir nazar is tarah
n dekha use jalvah-gar is tarah
magar gaah saaya sa mahtaab mein
kabhu vahm sa aa'lam-e khwaab mein

mujhe aap ko yuun hi khote gaaii
javaani tamaam apni sote gaaii
dikhaaya n us mah ne ruu khwaab mein
n dekha phir us ko kabhu khwaab mein
bahut be-khud o be-khabar ho chuka
ham aaghosh-e taal'e bahut so chuka
lagi jaan si aane aa'zaa ke biich
koi roz rahna tha duniya ke biich
n dekha kabhu Mir phir vo jamaal
vo sohbat thi goya k khwaab o khayal

The moment I left Akbarabaad,
I looked at the walls and portals with my tear-filled eyes.
How would I leave the place that belongs to me?
How should I make my heart behave
like a stone, every step of the way?
My afflicted heart cried out loudly.
In this act of leaving, my heart too left me.
My heart sheds blood, suffering the cruelty of the heavens.
Slowly and gradually, I was possessed by madness.

At night, I looked at the moon, and I was struck.
It was like some lightning that hit me.
I had a new kind of dream.
I saw her wherever my eyes turned,
the same visage in thousands of places.
Wherever I saw that mystifying figure
was the place to spend my entire years.

I looked—my eyes started shedding tears of blood.
If I could look at my condition,

it was as if a doomsday for my heart.
Sometimes, she appeared as a frame on the wall.
Sometimes, I saw her in wondrous motion.
Sometimes, she put her feet out of the frame in grand style.
Sometimes, she showed me her attractive countenance.
Sometimes, she covered her face with her tresses.
Sometimes, she placed her hands around my neck,
and then abruptly making it look like a hostile act.
For some nights at a stretch, this was the state of affairs.
Our association lasted for quite a while in this act of make-belief.

At last, healers were called in to look at my condition.
If a distasteful herb was prescribed, I had to sip it down the throat.
I was afraid of myself; I was in a state of senselessness.
A troubled heart; and a state of total despondency.
I was locked into a small cell to diminish the fire of my madness.
People were afraid to come close to me,
thinking I could harm them.

Things slowly showed some improvement,
and the condition that prevailed gradually subsided.
The deception of that image and the madness.
She showed some signs of estrangement.
She didn't give me the same old look of affection.
Poor thing, she started hitting her head against the wall.
Sometimes offering comfort, sometimes troubled.
Sometimes she was out of control in my pursuit.
Sometimes she showed her heart to me.
Sometimes she taunted me about my lack of constancy.
Sometimes she said farewell, goodbye.
Sorrow had sapped all my strength.

I never saw her again.
I never saw her in her glory again.
But sometimes a shadow in the moon;
sometimes a flicker of imagination in the world of dreams.

In a state of sleeplessness, I spent my youth losing you.
That moon-faced beauty didn't show her face in a dream.
I didn't see her in a dream ever again.
I lost my sense of awareness and self-consciousness.
I suffered due to my bad luck
but slowly, I regained my energy
because I had to live in the world for some more time.
Mir never saw that magnificent beauty again.
Was that a real thing, or the glow of my imagination, a dream?

Mir's poetry is filled with a celebration of love, its joy and trance, pain and enchantment. Here are some couplets that reflect the deep distress of his heart, including the creation of dreamlike images.

sub-h voh aafat uth baitha tha tum ne n dekha sad afsos
kya kya fitne sar jore palkon ke saaye saaye gaye

That calamity woke up early morning and
if you didn't notice, it was your bad luck.
What havoc must have passed under the shadow
of her eyelashes!

ji chahata hai a'ish karein ek raat ham
tu hove chaandni ho gulaabi sharaab ho

One night, I want to have a time of my life.
Your glorious presence, moonlight and rosy wine!

mausam-e abr ho subu bhi ho
gul ho gulshan ho aur tu bhi ho

A cloudy sky and a decanter of wine.
A rose garden, and just you!

qurbaan pyaala-e mai-e naab
jis se k tera hijaab nikla

Glory be to the cup of vintage wine
that helped in lifting your veil!

sabr kahaan jo tum ko kahiye lag ke gale se so jao
bolo n bolo baitho n baitho khare khare tuk ho jao

No patience to tell you, come and sleep in my embrace.
No need to say anything, no need to take any trouble,
just be still in the moment!

jab milne ka savaal karuun huun zulf o rukh dikhlaate ho
barson mujhko yuun hi guzre sub-h o shaam bataate ho

When I ask you about meeting,
you show me your locks and looks.
I have spent years waiting.
You keep saying, this morning, that evening.

lete hi naam us ka sote se chaonk uthe
hai khair Mir sahib kuchh tum ne kwaab dekha

Someone uttered her name and suddenly you woke up.
Are you all right, Mir sahib? Were you in a dream state?

The mid-1750s were a challenging time for people living
in Delhi. Four Mughal emperors occupied the throne
between 1719 and 1760. Each one of them was either killed
or overthrown. Nadir Shah's invasion in 1739 crippled the
city. But a greater calamity befell when Ahmad Shah Abdali,
another barbarian invader, conquered north India in 1747.
Abdali attacked eight times, and each invasion left behind
a tale of great pillage and devastation. Mir devotes a large
portion of *Zikr-e Mir* describing these invasions and wars as
well as his acquaintances with the main characters involved in
these calamities.

Mir left Delhi for Lucknow in 1782 when Shah Alam II
was the Mughal emperor. The British consolidated their
presence in Delhi by 1803, three years before the emperor's
death. Asaf-ud Daula, the ruler of Awadh, Mir's patron in
Lucknow, was more a vassal of the English than the emperor
in Delhi. The nawab was known for his erratic temperament
and led a life of luxury and pleasure. Their relationship soured
soon and Mir stopped visiting the nawab's residence for
poetry recitations. The time Mir spent in Lucknow between
1782, when he arrived from Delhi, and 1810, when he passed
away, is not covered in *Zikr-e Mir*. Not much is known about
his life in the city other than episodes narrated in different
tazkirahs.

One exciting and fascinating source for some of the famous episodes about Mir's obsession with his self-esteem and unusual behaviour towards others is Mohammad Husain Azad and his book *Aab-e Hayaat*, published nearly a hundred years later. Azad's book is unique in the sense that it was the first scholarly history of hundreds of classical Urdu poets written in literary prose. The book stands in sharp contrast to tazkirahs, which were cursory and written in the format of chronicles with short personal comments. *Aab-e Hayaat* documents several episodes from Mir's life, especially after he moved to Lucknow, revealing many facets of his complex personality that are not available anywhere else. At the outset, Azad pays Mir the highest compliment, stating that in the world of poetry, he was nothing less than a sparkling sun. His admirers treated his work in the same way as they looked upon diamonds and pearls. They spread the poet's name around like one disperses perfume. 'He was the only Rekhta poet of Dilli whose ghazals were carried by the travellers as a gift from one city to another.'[4]

Azad describes an interesting incident during Mir's travel to Lucknow by a bullock cart. Because Mir did not have the money to arrange a cart for his exclusive use, he agreed to share it with another passenger. The two of them exchanged pleasantries, but then Mir turned his face to the other side. The co-passenger tried to start a conversation but failed. As the passenger tried again, Mir retorted, 'Sahib, you have paid the fare for travel. It does not include a conversation with me.'

4   Mohammad Husain Azad, *Aab-e Hayaat* (Lahore: Malik Azad Book Depot, n.d.), p. 204.

The person replied, 'But what is the harm in a conversation? Talking eases the boredom of travel.' Irritated by this persistent questioning, Mir responded, 'It may be your pleasure, but it spoils my idiom.'[5]

As Mir reached the outskirts of Lucknow, he might have made a stopover in a sarai. He came to know that a mushaira was being held in the city. He wrote a ghazal and joined other poets on the stage. But his unusually formal attire—a sword, a lancet, and pointed shoes—evoked remarks by onlookers. Mir was tired and disheartened because of travel stress and the grief of leaving Delhi, a city that he loved very much. He didn't say anything and sat in a corner. When his turn came, the host asked him to say a few words about his whereabouts. Mir read the heart-rending couplets of the following *qat'a* (thematically integrated couplets) to start his recitation that beautifully captured devastation of Delhi and explained why he was in Lucknow.

kya buud o baash puuchho ho puurab ke saakino
ham ko ghariib jaan ke hans hans pukaar ke

Dilli jo ek shahr tha aa'lam mein intikhaab
rehte the muntakhab hi jahaan rozgaar ke

us ko falak ne luut ke viraan kar diya
ham rahne vaale hain usi ujre diyaar ke

---

5   Ibid., p. 205.

How can I tell you my whereabouts, O residents of the East?
You consider me an alien as you laughingly inquire about my
whereabouts.

Dilli was once considered one of the finest cities in the world,
and only cultured and highly sophisticated people lived there.

The heavens robbed it and devastation followed.
I am a resident of the same ruined place.

When people came to know that the unknown poet was Mir
Taqi Mir, they offered apologies. By the next morning, the
news that Mir had arrived in Lucknow spread throughout the
city. The ruling nawab Asif-ud Daula fixed a monthly pension
of rupees two hundred for the poet as a welcome gesture.[6]

Mir's relationship with nawab started on a good note, but
it did not last very long because, unlike many other poets, Mir
would not compromise his honour and dignity for silver or
gold coins. Azad narrates an exciting encounter between the
two. One day, the nawab sent for Mir, who showed up at the
palace as desired. The nawab was standing near a pond that
had small fish of different colours and hues. He had a fancy
cane in his hands, which he used to poke and prod the fish.
Although he asked Mir to recite, the nawab's attention was
divided. Mir read a few couplets and then stopped. When the
nawab asked Mir to continue reading, Mir could not resist
the urge to question the nawab's etiquette as poets are given
full attention when they read their verse. 'How can I continue

---

6   Ibid., pp. 205–06.

to read, Nawab Sahib, when you are busy playing with the fish?' The nawab replied, 'When I hear a good couplet, it will automatically get my attention.' Mir did not like the response. He left the palace.[7]

Azad narrates an exchange between Mir and some of his contemporaries in Lucknow that throws light on his self-esteem as a master poet. Someone asked, 'Hazrat, who do you think are the true poets of today?' Mir said that there were not more than two and mentioned the name of Sauda and his own, calling himself *khaaksaar* (humble, modest). He paused and then added, 'Maybe we can treat Khwaja Mir Dard as half a poet. That makes two and one-half, that's all!'

'Sir! What about Mir Soz?' someone inquired.

Showing his displeasure, Mir answered, 'Is he a poet?'

The person said, 'But you know, he is the court poet of Nawab Sahib.'

Mir paused for a moment, then added, 'If that is so, maybe, take him as one-fourth a poet. That makes two and three-quarters, and that's it.'

One day, some of Lucknow's learned people showed up at Mir's house. They were received by the poet's maid and offered hookah. Mir appeared after some time and joined them. Following the exchange of pleasantries, the visitors, with due respect, requested for some *kalaam* (poetry) as was customary. Mir avoided the subject and asked to be excused. But when the visitors insisted, Mir said bluntly, 'You will not appreciate my poetry.'

---

[7]   Ibid., pp. 206–07.

The guests did not like the comment and responded, 'If we can appreciate the poetry of Anwari and Khaqani, why not yours?

Mir replied, 'Compendiums and lexicons are available to appreciate their crafty poetry. But for my poetry one must know the idiom of the heart of Dilli, and an experience of sitting on the steps of Jam'a Masjid, which you are deprived of. You look for trivialities and verbosity that are found in heavy volumes, but that is not my way. I know only the chaste idiom of Dilli, and that is not your privilege. I would like to be excused.' The meeting ended on that disconcerting note.[8]

By the time Nawab Saadat Ali Khan's reign started after Asif-ud Daula passed away, Mir had already stopped going to the royal court. One day, Nawab Saadat Ali Khan's entourage was passing through the street. Mir was sitting on the steps of the famous Tahsiin mosque. On seeing the nawab, everyone stood up but Mir. The nawab asked Insha, the poet, who was in attendance, 'Who was that person who didn't show me respect?' Insha mentioned Mir's name circuitously and reminded the nawab that they had previously talked about him. He was now living in extreme poverty. The nawab sent one thousand rupees through a royal messenger as a gift. On seeing the money, Mir lost his temper and told the messenger, 'You can give it to a mosque.' Later, at the request of the nawab, Insha came to see Mir and told him that he should not refuse the king's gift. Mir was adamant. He replied, 'The king is that of a country. But I am also king of a country (meaning the world of poetry). Is it proper protocol in relationships to

---

8   Ibid., pp. 218–19.

send money through messengers?' Insha's persuasive skills however, won the day, and the matter was resolved. Mir started going to the royal court. In due course, he became the nawab's favourite poet.[9]

Mir passed away in 1810. His *Kulliyaat* (Collected Works) were published a year later by the Fort Williams College in Calcutta, a significant event that the poet did not live to witness himself.

rang-e gul o buu-e gul hote hain hava donon
kya kaafila jaata hai jo tu bhi chala chaahe

The colours of roses and the fragrance of flowers fade away.
What a caravan departs as you leave!

---

[9]   Ibid., pp. 219–20.

Part I

Selected Ghazals

Let's Go to the Garden

dikhaaii diye yuun k be-khud kiya
hamein aap se bhi juda kar chale

When I saw you I lost my senses.
I was not in my body after I fell in love with you.

Mir Taqi Mir was not only Urdu's first great poet, he was also the most prolific. His complete poetical work spans six Divans, consisting of about 13,500 couplets. These are mainly ghazals, but they do cover other genres like masnavi, qasida, and rubai as well. Given the vastness of the poet's output, the task of making a selection of fifty ghazals is extremely challenging. We looked at the compilations of Mir by three highly respected scholars and distinguished Urdu writers, namely Mohammad Husain Azad, *Baaba-e Urdu* Maulvi Abdul Haq, and Nasir Kazmi. We concluded that such a selection would always be considered subjective, reflecting the taste of the person making the selection. There is a saying in Urdu: *pasand apni apni khayaal apna apna* (likes and preferences differ from one person to another). Ghalib once said, *'she'ron ke intikhaab ne rusva kiya mujhe'* (selection of couplets have earned me notoriety). Advances in literary theory and poetics maintain that each generation brings to the reading of a text their own horizons of expectations. Nonetheless, there is a common denominator that governs literary creations that are called masterpieces—pieces of prose and poetry that stand the test of time and stay evergreen. While making our selection of Mir ghazals, we have kept this in view.

Before we come to the analysis of and critical reflections about Mir's poetry, which follows in Part II of the book, we thought it was a good idea to give the reader a taste of Mir's ghazals. We shall argue and establish some distinguishing features of Mir's ingenious multidimensional creativity and his soul-stirring love poetry, but there is merit in exploring things on one's own rather than being guided by an expert. Mir was widely accepted as Khuda-e Sukhan who earned fame for his seventy-two nishtars. But this view was highly limiting. Mir has hundreds of good couplets that have this razor-sharp quality. The genre of the ghazal, it should be noted, is like a bouquet of multiple hues and colours. One couplet could be sharp and the other not so; one could express a yearning for the beloved, and the other manifest the pain and suffering of mankind or mourn the pillage of the poet's favourite city (Dilli in case of Mir). We can say with great confidence that the ghazals presented here will make you stop and think. They will lift your spirits, prodding you to be aware of the entirety of your being and your potential to go beyond the typically exhausting and mundane concerns of life.

In Part II of the book, we shall employ textual, objective, and scientific approach while looking at Mir's poetic work.

We shall challenge the conventional view that Mir was a simple, one-dimensional poet. He did use conversational idiom with a touch of the colloquial that might appear simple, but his simplicity was deceptive. Mir had a good command of Persian, and he blended it so well with the raw earthly idiom that his language became the standard for poets that followed him.

Firaq Gorakhpuri, the great progressive Urdu poet, played an essential role in reviving interest in Mir's poetry several years before partition. He found the elements of *sringara rasa* (the flavour of romantic love, also called the mother of all flavours in ancient Indian tradition) in Mir's poetry inspiring. He maintained that Mir's poetry echoed the voice of humankind. He wrote, 'When Mir puts his hand on his heart, we get the feeling that he has placed his hand on the heart of all humanity. Our Mir thus becomes Mir of the whole world.'[1] But the real revival of Mir's poetry occurred after partition. With massive killings, great devastation, and large-scale uprooting of people, in some ways, the pillage and ruination of Mir's Dilli was repeated many times over. Nasir Kazmi, an iconic poet, maintained that the night of Mir's lifetime had stretched itself and had become one with the dark night of our time. The undercurrent of deep pain, anguish, despondency, and suffering of Mir's poetry thus found a new voice among poets of the younger generation in both India and Pakistan. Two great singers of our time—Lata

---

[1]   Mir Taqi Mir, *Kulliyaat-e Mir,* vol. 1 (New Delhi: National Council for Promotion of Urdu Language, 2007), pp. 85–86.

Mangeshkar and Mehdi Hasan—have sung Mir's masterpiece ghazals which are included here.

Every great Urdu poet, including Ghalib, has written a couplet honouring Mir as a pioneer and a trailblazer. Here is a couplet by Zauq, Ghalib's contemporary and the court poet of the last Mughal king Bahadur Shah Zafar:

n hua par n hua Mir ka andaaz nasiib
Zauq yaaron ne bahut zor ghazal mein maara

We tried but were never able to capture Mir's voice, although Zauq and his friends achieved much in the field of ghazal writing.

1

chalte ho to chaman ko chaliye kahte hain k bahaaraan hai
paat hare hain phuul khile hain kam kam baad o baaraan hai

Let's go to the garden,
they say spring is here.
Leaves have turned green.
Flowers are blooming.
There is a whiff of breeze
and some drizzle.

rang hava se yuun tapke hai jaise sharaab chuvaate hain
aage ho maikhaane ke niklo a'hd-e baada gusaaraan hai

Gentle breeze is dripping colour,
just as wine is distilled.
Let us leave the tavern behind us;
and we should drink hard and long.

i'shq ke maidaan daaron mein bhi marne ka hai vasf bahut
yaa'ni musiibat aisi uthaana kaar-e kaar guzaaraan hai

Those who are engaged in the struggle of love
have the quality of dying readily.
Inviting self-annihilation with dignity
is the work of those who are brave hearts.

dil hai daagh jigar hai tukre aansu saare khuun hue
lohu paani ek kare y i'shq-e laala azaaraan hai

My heart is reduced to a scar
broken into pieces.
My tears have turned into drops of blood.
This is what falling in love
with those tulip-faced beauties does to you.
It obliterates the distinction between
blood and tears.

kohkan o majnun ki khaatir dasht o koh mein ham n gaye
i'shq mein ham ko Mir nihaayat paas-e izzat daaraan hai

Keeping in mind Farhad and Majnun,
I have avoided the barren lands and mountains.
In the realm of love, Mir has shown regard
to lovers who are worthy of great honour
and he has chosen a different path.

2

aaj hamaare ghar aaya to kya hai yaan jo nisaar karein
illa khench baghal mein tujh ko der talak ham pyaar karein

What a surprise that you have come
to visit me today in my home,
but I don't know what I can offer you.
I want to hold you in my arms
and express my love for a long time.

khaak hue barbaad hue paamaal hue sab mahv hue
aur shadaa-yid i'shq ki rah ke kaise ham hamvaar karein

I was reduced to dust and ruined.
I was trampled underfoot and
my being was destroyed.
How else I could have endured
the hardships that my love gave me!

sheva apna be-parvaaii nau-miidi se thahra hai
kuchh bhi vo maghruur dabe to mannat ham sau baar karein

Faced with utter desperation,
I have become indifferent to things.
I wish I knew how to confront
her haughtiness a little bit,
then I would bow before her
a hundred times.

ham to faqiir hain khaak baraabar aa baithe to lutf kya
nang-e jahaan lagta ho un ko vaan ve aisi aa'r karein

I am a mendicant
and my worth is no more than a pile of dust.
I come and sit here if it is your pleasure.
If your dignity is hurt in such situations,
feel free to tell me so.

patta patta gulshan ka to haal hamaara jaane hai
aur kahe to jis se ai gul be-bargi izhaar karein

Every leaf in the garden knows my state of mind.
Who should I tell my condition, O rose,
if not the greenery of this garden?

Mir ji hain ge ek jo aaye kya ham un se dard kahein
kuchh bhi jo sun paavein to y majlis mein bistaar karein

Mir is the one who comes to meet me,
but what can I tell him about my pain?
Even if he hears a little bit of what I have to say,
he will broadcast my tale of love in some detail.

3

arz o sama mein i'shq hai saari chaaron or bhara hai i'shq
ham hain janaab i'shq ke bande nazdik apne khuda hai i'shq

Love is in the earth and the sky.
All four directions are full of love.
Sir, I am a humble servant,
i'shq for me is no different than God.

zaahir o baatin avval o aakhir paaien baala i'shq hai sab
nuur o zulmat maa'ni o suurat sab kuchh aap hi hua hai i'shq

Visible and invisible, first and last,
below and above—
there is nothing else except *i'shq*.
Light and darkness, hidden and manifest—
i'shq embraces everything.

ek taraf jabriil aata hai ek taraf laata hai kitaab
ek taraf pinhaan hai dilon mein ek taraf paida hai i'shq

On one side Gabriel comes,
on the other he brings the Book.
On one side love is hidden in the hearts,
on the other it is manifest and seen by all.

khaak o baad o aaab o aatish sab hai mavaafiq apne ta-ien
jo kuchh hai so i'shq-e butaan hai kya kahiye ab kya hai i'shq

Earth, wind, water, and fire.
They are all complete in themselves.
Love above all is the love of the beloved.
Now, how can we say what is love?

Mir kahein hangaama aara main to nahien huun chaahat ka
sabr n mujh se kiya jaave to muaa'f rakho k naya hai i'shq

Mir says he is not caught up
in the commotion of love!
I can't control myself.
Not my fault actually
because I'm a new victim of love.

4

baat kya aadmi ki ban aaii
aasmaan se zamiin napvaaii

When man felt empowered,
he could not control his ego.
Next thing, he made the skies
bow to the earth.

maah o khurshiid o abr o baad sabhi
us ki khaatir hue hain saudaaii

The moon, the sun, clouds,
and the wind.
They are all deeply in love,
and they wander madly
struck with awe.

hairat aati hai us ki baatein dekh
khudsari khud sataaii khud-raaii

I am amazed watching him
how he behaves.
Egocentric, self-absorbed,
and domineering.

Mir naachiiz musht-e khaak allah
us ne y kibriyaa kahaan paaii

Humble Mir, lost in the love of God,
is no more than a handful of dust,
Who infused him with greatness?

5

baatein hamaari yaad rahein phir baatein aisi n suniye ga
parhte kisu ko suniye ga to der talak sar dhuniye ga

Do remember carefully what I have to say.
You won't hear such talk again.
If you hear someone recite like this,
you will be overwhelmed and wonderstruck
by the sheer ecstasy of my words.

sa'ii o talaash bahut si rahe gi is andaaz ke kahne ki
sohbat mein u'lma fuzala ki ja kar parihiye guniye ga

You will make much effort and you will try
many ways to say in this style.
You will seek the company of learned folks
to read and learn my form of expression.

dil ki tasalli jab k ho gi guft o shunuud se logon ki
aag phuke gi gham ki badan mein is mein jaliye bhuniye ga

When you will not be satisfied
with your exchanges with friends,
the fire of grief will overpower you.
Your body will burn and you will scorch
and roast too in this fire.

garm ash'aar Mir daruuna daaghon se y bhar dein ge
zard ru shahr mein phiriye ga galiyon mein ne gul chuniye ga

Mir's verse is so charged with fire
that it would fill your inner self
with marks that are dark and deep.
Showing your pale countenance,
you will wander in the city and its lanes
but will not find the roses of your choice.

6

band-e qaba ko khuubaan jis vaqt vaa karein ge
khamyaaza kash jo hon ge milne ke kya karein ge

When the beautiful idols
untie the knot of their apparel
and open their arms.
What a sight it will be
when they are cuddled
and embraced!

rona yahi hai mujh ko teri jafa se har dam
y dil dimaagh donon kab tak vafa karein ge

When I look at your infidelity,
I can't help but complain all the time.
How long my heart and mind
will continue to be loyal?

hai diin sar ka dena gardan p apni khuubaan
jiite hain to tumhaara y qarz adaa karein ge

To sacrifice this head for you
is part of my belief, O love!
If I continue to live,
surely, this debt will be repaid.

darvesh hain ham aakhir do ik nigeh ki rukhsat
goshe mein baithe pyaare tum ko dua karein ge

I am no better than a dervish.
You should not mind
if I look at you for a while.
I will sit in a corner, my dear,
and will pray for your wellbeing.

kuchh to kahe ga ham ko khaamosh dekh kar vo
is baat ke liye ab chup hi raha karein ge

She will say something
when she finds me waiting in silence.
For that reason alone,
I will remain silent and say nothing.

aa'lam mare hai tujh par aaii agar qayaamat
teri gali ke har su mahshar hua karein ge

The whole world loves you to death.
Wonder what will happens
on the day of resurrection!
There will be a lot of commotion
in and around your lane.

daamaan-e dasht suukha abron ki be-tahi se
jangal mein rone ko ab ham bhi chala karein ge

The forest is dry and withered
due to the indifference of clouds.
What a wonderful excuse for me
to seek a place in the jungle to cry!

laaii teri gali tak aavaargi hamaari
zillat ki apni ab ham i'zzat kiya karein ge

My wanderlust
finally brought me to your lane.
Now I will have to show respect
to my disgrace.

ahvaal Mir kyonkar aakhir ho ek shab mein
ik u'mr ham y qissa tum se kaha karein ge

How can Mir narrate his whole story
in one short evening?
I will be sharing this account with you
for the rest of my life.

7

dekh to dil k jaan se uth-ta hai
y dhuaan sa kahaan se uth-ta hai

Look at the source:
from where do the fumes arise?
Is it from the heart or the soul?
Some thing for sure is smouldering,
but from where does the smoke arise?

gor kis dil jale ki hai y falak
sho'la ik sub-h yaan se uth-ta hai

Whose grave is this, O sky! The cruel doer?
Does it belong to the one with a burnt-heart?
Each morning, I see a fierce flame rising.

khaana-e dil se ziinhaar n ja
koi aise makaan se uth-ta hai

The heart has a little dwelling place.
Don't move away from it.

Does anyone leave a home like this one?

larti hai us ki chashm-e shokh jahaan
ek aashob vaan se uth-ta hai

At the spot where her seductive eye
strikes someone,
there is ruination, calamity, and disaster.

baithne kaun de hai phir us ko
jo tere aastaan se uth-ta hai

The one who rises from your doorsteps
is not allowed to settle down
anywhere for the rest of his life.

yuun uthe aah us gali se ham
jaise koi jahaan se uth-ta hai

I left her alley
in an agony similar to the one
who is leaving this world.

i'shq ik Mir bhaari patthar hai
kab y tujh naa-tavaan se uth-ta hai

Passionate love is like
a heavy boulder, O Mir!
How a frail person like you
will ever be able to lift it.

8

dil baham pahuncha badan mein tab se saaraa tan jala
aa pari y aisi chingaari k pairaahan jala

Since the heart was placed inside,
the whole body has been burning and sweltering.
This was the spark, alas, that ignited the fire
destroying the whole warp and woof.

kab talak dhuuni lagaaye jogiyon ki si rahuun
baithe baithe dar p tere to mera aasan jala

How long should I sit like a yogi
in front of your house
burning a smoky fire,
and body smeared with ash?
Sitting in this posture for days
has set my mat up in flames.

suukhte hi aansuon ke nuur aankhon ka gaya
bujh hi jaate hain diye jis vaqt sab roghan jala

When my tears dried up,
my eyes went dark.
Lamps shed their light
when the fuel is finished.

sho'la afshaani nahien y kuchh naii is aah se
duun lagi hai aisi aisi bhi k saara ban jala

My fiery sighs are nothing new.
But they can do lot of damage.
Small hidden fires sometimes burn down
the entire forest.

aag si ik dil mein sulge hai kabhu bharki to Mir
de gi meri haddiyon ka dher juun iindhan jala

There is a fire in my heart, Mir,
that is smouldering.
If it ever gathered momentum,
it would reduce my bones
to a pile of ashes.

9

faqiiraana aaye sada kar chale
k miyaan khush raho ham du'aa kar chale

I came like a mendicant.
I made my call and left a prayer:
Miyan, be happy;
you have my blessings!
These were my words before I departed.

jo tujh bin n jiine ko kahte the ham
so is a'hd ko ab vafa kar chale

I told you
I could not live without you.
Now I fulfill my promise
by leaving this world.

koi na-ummiidaana karte nigaah
so tum ham se munh bhi chhupa kar chale

I would have been satisfied
with a despairing look,
but before you departed
you even veiled your face from me.

bahut aarzu thi gali ki teri
so yaan se luhu mein naha kar chale

I had great desire
to see your alley.
So I took a bath in blood
before I departed.

dikhaaii diye yuun k be-khud kiya
hamein aap se bhi juda kar chale

When I saw you
I lost my senses.
I was not in my body
after I fell in love with you.

jabiin sajde karte hi karte gaii
haq-e bandagi ham ada kar chale

Constant prostration
made a mark on my forehead.
But as your servant I did my part
before I departed.

parastish ki yaan tak ki ai but tujhe
nazar mein sabhon ki khuda kar chale

My adoration for you, my idol,
crossed all limits.
I turned you into a divine deity
before I departed.

gaaii u'mr dar band fikr-e ghazal
so is fan ko aisa bara kar chale

I spent my whole life
in the service of ghazal
and raising this art
to the pinnacle of excellence!

kahein kya jo puuchhe koi ham se Mir
jahaan mein tum aaye the kya kar chale

What should I tell, Mir,
if someone asks:
You came into this world.
What did you do
before you departed?

10

garche kab dekhte ho par dekho
aarzu hai k tum idhar dekho

Although you never look at me,
I request you to do so now.
This is my intense desire.
I want you to listen
to my entreaties.

i'shq kya kya hamein dikhaata hai
aah tum bhi to ik nazar dekho

Love makes us vulnerable.
Please do come closer and
look at the wonder.

yuun a'rq jalvagar hai us munh par
jis tarah os phuul par dekho

Her face glows when she perspires
and traces of sweat appear on her face,
just like dewdrops on a flower.

pahunche hain ham qariib marne ke
yaa'ni jaate hain duur agar dekho

I have reached a point
where I am ready to depart.
I will go very far.
Think about it and look at me.

lutf mujh mein bhi hain hazaaron Mir
diidni huun jo soch kar dekho

I am filled with
countless delights, Mir.
I am worth a look
if you observe me
as intently as you can.

11

ham aap hi ko apna maqsuud jaante hain
apne sivaae kis ko maujuud jaante hain

I consider myself
to be the focus of my search.
No one, but I am the only one
who exists.

a'jz o niyaaz apna apni taraf hai saara
is musht-e khaak ko ham masjuud jaante hain

All my humility and consideration
is directed towards my own self.
Though it is no more than a handful of dust,
it is worthy of dedication and devotion.

i'shq un ki a'ql ko hai jo maasaavaa hamaare
naachiiz jaante hain naabuud jaante hain

If according to their wisdom
something other than the self
is worthy of veneration,
they have no worth or substance.

apni hi sair karne ham jalvaagar hue the
is ramz ko valekin maa'duud jaante hain

We came to this world
to explore the reality of self.
This great secret is known only
to very few people.

mar kar bhi haath aave to Mir muft hai vo
ji ke ziyaan ko bhi ham suud jaante hain

If I get her while dying, Mir,
she will cost me nothing.
All the tribulations in the business of love
are actually a gain.

12

hasti apni habaab ki si hai
y numaaish saraab ki si hai

This life is no different from a bubble.
This showmanship, this exhibition,
is no different from a mirage.

nazuki us ke lab ki kya kahiye
pankhari ik gulaab ki si hai

What can anyone say
about the delicate beauty of her lips?
They are more like a petal of a rose.

baar baar us ke dar p jaata huun
haalat ab iztiraab ki si hai

I go to her door time and again,
notwithstanding the mental state
that shows my great distress.

main jo bola kaha k y aavaaz
usi khaana-kharaab ki si hai

On hearing my voice she said:
this voice belongs
to the ruinous person
whom I know and recognize.

Mir un niim-baaz aankhon mein
saari masti sharaab ki si hai

Mir, the intoxication
of those half-opened eyes
is exactly the same
that comes from wine.

13

jis sar ko ghuruur aaj hai yaan taajvari ka
kal us p yahiin shor hai phir nauha-gari ka

The one who is proud
of wearing a crown today,
he will soon see a day of lamentation
hit him tomorrow.

aafaaq ki manzil se gaya kaun salaamat
asbaab luta raah mein yaan har safari ka

No one has traversed this universe safely.
Everyone had his belongings plundered,
somewhere on the way.

zindaan mein bhi shorish n gaii apne junuun ki
ab sang madaava hai is aashufta-sari ka

Even the prison could not cure
the tumult of my madness.

Now the only cure left is a stone
to dash my crazy head against.

le saans bhi aahista k naazuk hai bahut kaam
aafaaq ki is kaar-gah-e shiisha-gari ka

Breathe carefully; it is a delicate task.
This illusory world in real terms
is a glassmaker's workshop.

tuk Mir-e jigar sokhta ki jald khabar le
kya yaar bharosa hai chiraagh-e saheri ka

Get some news about Mir
whose heart is on fire.
You can't depend on the lamp
that has burnt overnight
and the morning is near.

14

kis ki masjid kaise maikhaane kahaan ke sheikh o shaab
ek gardish mein teri chashm-e siyaah ke sab kharaab

Who cares for the mosque? What taverns?
Where are the sheikhs and the reckless youth?
When you look around with your beautiful dark eyes,
they all tumble over, badly drunk, with one look.

mond rakhna chashm ka hasti mein aa'iin-e diid hai
kuchh nahien aata nazar jab aankh khole hai habaab

Keeping the eyes closed in this life
is a good way of seeing the enigmatic world.
Nothing is visible when the bubble
opens its eyes; it simply bursts!

tu ho aur duniya ho saaqi main huun masti ho mudaam
par bat-e sehba nikaale ur chale rang sharaab

In your and wine-pourer's company
lies my whole world
and my everlasting intoxication.
Let the duck open its wings
and let the colour of wine fly everywhere.

mat dhalak mizhgaan se ab to ae sirishk-e aabdaar
muft mein jaati rahe gi teri moti ki si aab

Don't fall down from my eyelashes,
O my sparkling tear.
You will lose your pearl-like
lustrous shine for zilch.

kuchh nahien bahr-e jahaan ki mauj par mat bhuul Mir
duur se dariya nazar aata hai lekin hai saraab

It is nothing, Mir.
Don't get deceived
by the high waves of the world.
What you see as a river
from the distance
is nothing but a mirage.

15

kuchh mauj-e hava pechaan ae Mir nazar aaii
shaayad k bahaar aaii zanjiir nazar aaii

The wave of breeze
appeared to me, Mir,
swaying and dancing.
Probably I saw the spring.
Or was it a chain?

dilli ke n the kuuche auraaq-e musavvar the
jo shakl nazar aaii tasviir nazar aaii

The lanes of Dilli were not lanes.
They were more like pages from an album.
Every face that you saw was like
a magnificent heart-stopping image.

maghruur bahut the ham aansu ki saraayit par
so sub-h ke hone ko taasiir nazar aaii

I was very proud
about the effect that my tears could create.
When morning came
there was proof for everyone to see.

gul baar kare hai ga asbaab-e safar shaayad
ghunche ki tarah bulbul dilgiir nazar aaii

The rose is probably packing things for travel.
The bud and the nightingale saw it and
they both were forlorn and heartbroken.

us ki to dil-aazaari be-hiich hi thi yaaro
kuchh ham ko hamaari bhi taqsiir nazar aaii

Her effort to make me suffer, dear friends,
was futile, without any real damage.
But there was some deficiency on my part too.

16

kya kahuun tum se main k kya hai i'shq
jaan ka rog hai bala hai i'shq

What can I tell you
how to define passionate love?
It is a soul's affliction;
it is a calamity.

i'shq hi i'shq hai jahaan dekho
saare aa'lam mein bhar raha hai i'shq

There is intense love
wherever you look.
The whole world
is filled with fervent love.

i'shq hai tarz o taur i'shq ke ta-iin
kahien banda kahien khuda hai i'shq

Love is its own praise.
Somewhere ordinary, human,
in other places God and Love
are no different

i'shq maa'shuuq i'shq aa'shiq hai
yaa'ni apna hi mubtala hai i'shq

Love is beloved.
It is the lover too.
Love is itself and
the one it engages.

dilkash aisa kahaan hai dushman-e jaan
mudd'aii hai p mudd'aa hai i'shq

It is tempting and irresistible
to the extent of being an enemy of life.
Love is the subject as well as the very object
of one's being.

Mir ji zard hote jaate ho
kya kahien tum ne bhi kiya hai i'shq

Dear Mir, you are getting paler
by each passing day.
Have you also fallen in love?

17

lazzat se nahien khaali jaanon ka khapa jaana
kab khizr o masiiha ne marne ka maza jaana

It is not without pleasure
that so many lives are lost.
Did Khizr or Jesus enjoy
the ecstasy of dying?

y bhi hai ada koi khurshiid namat pyaare
munh sub-h dikha jaana phir shaam chhupa jaana

What style is this, my dear, that just like the sun,
you show your face in the morning and
then go into hiding when evening comes?

kab bandagi meri si banda kare ga koi
jaane hai khuda us ko main tujh ko khuda jaana

No one can practice devotion like me.
If there is one such, God knows him.
But for me you are my God.

tha naaz bahut ham ko daanist par apni bhi
aakhir vo bura nikla ham jis ko bhala jaana

I was very vain
about my wisdom and understanding.
But someone I trusted to be good
turned out to be bad.

dhab dekhne ka iidhar aisa hi tumhaara tha
jaate to ho par ham se tuk aankh mila jaana

How to explain
the way you looked at me?
If you are leaving,
just look me in the eye once.

ae shor-e qayaamat ham sote hi n rah jaavein
is raah se nikle to ham ko bhi jaga jaana

O tumult of the doomsday,
don't leave me behind while I'm sleeping.
When you pass this way,
make sure that you wake me up.

jaati hai guzar ji par us waqt qayaamat si
yaad aave hai jab tera yak-baargi aa jaana

My heart suffers
doomsday-like affliction

when I remember
your coming over to see me.

barson se mere us ki rahti hai yahi sohbat
tegh us ko uthaana to sar mujh ko jhuka jaana

It has been the state of affairs
for years now.
She picks up a sword
and I lower my head.

kab Mir basar aaye tum vaise farebi se
dil ko to laga baithe lekin n laga jaana

How can you put up, Mir,
with that kind of artful trickster?
You have fallen in love,
but you never knew
what this affliction was.

18

Mir dariya hai sune she'r zabaani us ki
allah allah re tabiyaa't ki ravaani us ki

Mir resembles a river.
We have heard him recite.
By the grace of God,
his temperament
is a gush of creativity.

miinh to bauchhaar ka dekha hai baraste tum ne
isi andaaz se thi ashk fashaani us ki

You may have seen
the powerful rain shower.
The way he cried uncontrollably
was no different.

baat ki tarz ko dekho to koi jaadu tha
par mili khaak mein kya sehr bayaani us ki

The style of his conversation
was really enchanting.
But his magical capabilities
dissolved into dust.

sar-guzasht apni kis andoh se shab kehta tha
so gaye tum n suni aah kahaani us ki

Last evening,
he was telling his story
with great grief.
But you fell asleep.
Alas, you didn't hear his tale
of heart-rending woe.

marsiye dil ke kaii kah ke diye logon ko
shahr dilli mein hai sab paas nishaani us ki

He composed heartfelt elegies
and gave them to his friends.
In the city of Dilli everyone
has them as his imprint.

aable ki si tarah thes lagi phuut bahe
dard-mandi mein gaii saari javaani us ki

He was hit like a blister
and the wound leaked.
He spent all his life
in distress and suffering.

ab gaye us ke juz afsos nahien kuchh haasil
haif sad haif k kuchh qadr n jaani us ki

He is gone and
there is nothing to be gained
by grieving about it.
Pity, one hundred pities,
no one really valued him.

19

patta patta buuta buuta haal hamaara jaane hai
jaane n jaane gul hi n jaane baagh to saara jaane hai

Every leaf, every little plant,
knows my state of mind.
Only the rose does not know it,
but the whole garden knows.

charaagari bimaari-e dil ki rasm-e shehr-e husn nahien
varna dilbar naadaan bhi us dard ka chaara jaane hai

In the city where beauty resides,
there is no custom of curing heart's affliction.
Otherwise, even the unaware beloved
would have known how to provide relief.

aa'shiq to murda hai hamesha ji uth-ta hai dekhe use
yaar ke aa jaane ko yakayak u'mr dobaara jaane hai

A lover is dead
but he regains life on seeing her.
The very act of a beloved's sudden visit
is like gaining new life.

20

sabr kahaan jo tum ko kahiye lag ke gale se so jaao
bolo n bolo baitho n baitho khare khare tuk ho jaao

No patience to tell you,
come and fall asleep in my embrace.
No need to say anything,
no need to take any trouble.
Just be still in the moment!

barse hai ghurbat si ghurbat gor ke uuper aa'shiq ki
abr namat jo aao idhar to dekh ke tum bhi ro jaao

Utter desolation is pervading
over the lover's grave
and it is wreaking havoc.
If you come here like the cloud,
even you will cry a lot.

21

u'mr bhar ham rahe sharaabi se
dil-e pur-khuun ki ik gulaabi se

I was inebriated most of my life.
A little pink goblet filled with blood
simply stayed on my heart forever.

ji da-ha jaaye hai saher se aah
raat guzre gi kis kharaabi se

Alas! My heart is crestfallen
since the morning.
I wonder how awful
the night would be.

khilna kam kam kali ne siikha hai
us ki aankhon ki niim-khwaabi se

The bud opens slowly, very slowly.
Who do you think she learnt it from?

From my beloved's half-open
and dreamy eyes, of course.

burqa uth-te hi chaand sa nikla
daagh huun us ki be-hijaabi se

When she uncovered her face
I saw a moon rise.
The dazzle of her shimmering beauty
hit my heart and it left a scar.

kaam the i'shq mein bahut par Mir
ham hain faarigh hue shataabi se

There was a lot to be done in love, Mir,
but my luck did not get an opportunity
and I lost everything.

22

yaaro mujhe m'uaaf rakho main nashe mein huun
ab do to jaam khaali hi do main nashe mein huun

Friends, please excuse me
because I am inebriated.
If you give me a glass of wine,
give it totally empty.
You know I am drunk.

maa'zuur huun jo paaon mera be-tarah pare
tum sargraan to mujh se n ho main nashe mein huun

My apologies
if my walk is little out of step.
Please do not be unhappy with me.
You know I am drunk.

bhaagi namaaz-e jum'a to jaati nahien hai kuchh
chalta huun main bhi tuk to raho main nashe mein huun

The time of Friday prayers comes rushing,
but it is not going to run away anywhere.
I will come along if you wait a bit.
You know I am drunk.

naazuk mizaaj aap qayaamat hain Mir ji
juun shiisha mere munh n lago main nashe mein huun

Dear illustrious Mir,
you have a terrible temperament,
very volatile indeed.
Do not come close to me
as a wine cup touches lips.
It can get smashed.
You know I am drunk.

23

koft se jaan lab p aaii hai
ham ne kya chot dil p khaaii hai

I am fatigued and shattered
to the point of breaking down.
What a severe blow
my heart has received!

likhte ruq'a likhe gaye daftar
shauq ne baat kya barhaaii hai

I wanted to write a love note,
but I filled a whole lot of registers.
My desire for you really made it
a big deal.

aarzu us buland o baala ki
kya bala mere sar p laaii hai

Constant longing for that tall
and swaying beauty!
What a spell have I cast upon myself!

diidni hai shikastagi dil ki
kya i'maarat ghamon ne dhaaii hai

The breaking of the heart
is worth looking.
What a beautiful edifice
this calamity has brought down.

hai tasann'o k la'l hain vo lab
yaa'ni ik baat si banaaii hai

To say her lips are like crimson ruby
is simply a play of words.
They have no match, indeed.

dil se nazdiik aur itna duur
kis se us ko kuchh aashnaaii hai

She is close to the heart
yet she is far away.
Whoever knows her,
shares the same experience.

marg-e majnun p a'qal gum hai Mir
kya divaane ne maut paaii hai

The death of Majnun, Mir
makes me lose myself in disbelief.
Can a lover like him ever die?

24

kal baare ham se us se mulaaqaat ho gaii
do do bachan ke hone mein ik baat ho gaii

Yesterday,
I encountered her by chance.
We exchanged a few words
and believe me
what a talk it was.

kin kin musiibaton se hui sub-h shaam-e hijr
so zulfein hi banaate use raat ho gaii

What afflictions
I had to bear during the night
of separation!
She spent time
trying to arrange her tresses
until it was late
in the night.

gardish nigaah-e mast ki mauquuf saaqiya
masjid to sheikh ji ki kharabaat ho gaii

Saqi, please stop looking
with those dream-like enticing eyes.
The mosque of the esteemed Sheikh
has already turned into a place
crowded with intoxicated people.

apne to honth bhi n hile us ke ru b ru
ranjish ki vajah Mir vo kya baat ho gaii

I did not even open my lips
while I stood before her face to face.
Mir doesn't know what happened,
why she got upset without any reason.

25

ae nukiile y thi kahaan ki ada
khub gaii ji mein teri baanki ada

O bright and sharp one,
what kind of affectation is this?
Your delicate gesture entered my heart
just like a dagger.

jaadu karte hain ik nigaah ke biich
haae re chashm-e dilbaraan ki ada

They cast a spell
with just one glance.
Alas, the heart tearing looks of beloveds!

baat kahne mein gaaliyaan de hai
sunte ho mere badzubaan ki ada

Her speech gives the impression
she is calling names.

Did you hear what the one
with a wily tongue just said?

dil chale jaaye hain khiraam ke saath
dekhi chalne mein in butaan ki ada

She is strolling
with great abandon.
Just notice the charm
of her carefree sauntering.

khaak mein mil ke Mir ham samjhe
be-adaaii thi assmaan ki ada

Mir, I was reduced to ash
and then I understood.
The sky's way was full of
calamities for me.

26

gul o bulbul bahaar mein dekha
ek tujh ko hazaar mein dekha

I saw blossoms and nightingales
when the spring arrived.
Among one thousand others,
you were the only one
that captured my heart.

jal gaya dil safed hain aankhein
y to kuchh intizaar mein dekha

My heart was burnt.
My eyes have turned white.
I saw it happen while I waited
and waited for you.

jaisa muztar tha zindagi mein dil
vohien main ne qaraar mein dekha

The way it was anguished in life,
my heart was the same
while I was in a state of equanimity.

jin balaaon ko Mir sunte the
un ko is rozgaar mein dekha

The stories of calamities
that you had only heard, Mir,
you also saw them
in the real world.

27

jiite ji kuucha-e dildaar se jaaya n gaya
us ki diivaar ka sar se mere saaya n gaya

While I was alive I spent
all my time in the alley of my beloved.
The shadow of her wall
stayed with me forever.

vo to kal der talak dekhta iidhar ko raha
ham se hi haal-e tabaah apna dikhaaya n gaya

Yesterday, she continued to look towards me
for a long time. My bad luck!
I was not able to show my ruined state to her.

khaak tak kuuch-e dildaar ki chhaani ham ne
justuju ki p dil-e gum shuda paaya n gaya

I hit the dust of my beloved's street many times.
I searched for long
but my tormented heart was not found anywhere.

aatish-e tez judaaii mein yaka-yak us bin
dil jala yuun k tinuk ji bhi jalaaya n gaya

In the flames of separation,
my heart burnt so quickly
that my soul could not be burnt
the same way.

ji mein aata hai k kuchh aur bhi mauzuun kiije
dard-e dil ek ghazal mein to sunaya n gaya

A desire shows up within me
to search for a fresh new opening.
The story of my heart's grief
could not be told in just one ghazal.

28

dil a'jab shahr tha khayaalon ka
luuta maara hai husn vaalon ka

Heart is a strange city
of thoughts.
Looted and devastated
by the beautiful.

ji ko janjaal dil ko hai uljhaao
yaar ke halqa halqa baalon ka

My mind is caught up in a mesh
and there is a twist in my heart
caused by layers upon layers
of locks of my beloved.

n kaha kuchh n aa phira n mila
kaya jawaab in mere savaalon ka

She didn't say a word;
she didn't turn back
nor did she meet me.
What a way to answer
all my questions!

dam n le us ki zulfon ka maara
Mir kaata jiye n kaalon ka

The one who is seized
by her black tresses
will not wait
for his next breath.
Mir, a black snake bite,
as they say,
is the end of your life.

29

dil jo tha ik aabla phuuta gaya
raat ko siina bahut kuuta gaya

Something that was my heart
broke apart like a blister.
Last night, my chest
was beaten badly in desperation.

taa-ir-e rang-e hina ki si tarah
dil n us ke haath se chhuuta gaya

Like a henna-coloured bird,
I could not free my heart
from her grip.

main n kahta tha k munh kar dil ki or
ab kahaan vo aaiina tuuta gaya

I used to exhort you
to look inside your heart.

That mirror is now broken.
You can't find it anywhere.

dil ki viiraani ka kya mazkuur hai
y nagar sau martaba luuta gaya

Let us not talk about
the devastation of the heart.
This town was looted
numerous times.

Mir kis ko ab dimaagh-e guftgu
u'mr guzri rekhta chhuta gaya

Mir, who is left with
the art of saying things sweetly?
An age has passed
since I gave up on Rekhta.
No masters remain anymore.

30

dair o haram se guzre ab dil hai ghar hamaara
hai khatm is aable par sair o safar hamaara

I have been through temples and mosques,
but now my heart is my home.
With that blister my journey
has come to an end.

kuuche mein us ke ja kar banta nahien phir aana
khuun ek din gire ga us khaak par hamaara

When anyone goes to her alley,
he does not find a way to get back.
One day you will see
my blood sprinkled on that dust.

is karvaan sara mein kya Mir baar kholein
yaan kuuch lag raha hai shaam o saher hamaara

In this caravan of life, Mir,
what is the urgency to open your bags.
Departures take place here,
every evening and morning each day.

31

i'shq hamaare khayal para hai khwaab gaya aaraam gaya
ji ka jaana thahar raha hai sub-h gaya yaa shaam gaya

Love is in my thoughts,
I am losing my dreams and my comforts.
It is a matter of time my heart too will be gone—
be it in the morning or in the evening.

i'shq kiya so diin gaya iimaan gaya islaam gaya
dil ne aisa kaam kiya kuchh jis se main naakaam gaya

I fell in love. Lost my faith,
lost my creed and lost my religion.
My heart did something so strange
that I lost it all.

haae javaani kya kya kahiye shor saron mein rakhte the
ab kya hai vo a'hd gaya vo mausam vo hangaam gaya

When I was young I was so involved
in the clamour and commotion of life.
What is left now?
That age, that climate, that tumult of youth—
all is gone.

likhna kehna tark hua tha aapis mein to muddat se
ab jo qaraar kiya hai dil se khat bhi gaya paighaam gaya

For a long time now,
we were not writing
or speaking to each other.
With the new pact with my heart,
there will be no exchange
of letters or messages—
all is gone.

32

gul ko mahbuub ham qiyaas kiya
farq nikla bahut jo baas kiya

I thought of you
when I saw the rose
but when I smelled it,
there was a lot of difference.

kuchh nahien suujhta hamein us bin
shauq ne ham ko be-havaas kiya

I can't think of anything
without her.
My desire has taken away
my ability to think clearly.

i'shq mein ham hue n divaane
qais ki aabru ka paas kiya

I didn't lose my mind in love
as a mark of respect for Majnun.

sub-h tak sham'a sar ko dhunti rahi
kya patange ne iltmaas kiya

The candle was ecstatic
and flickering
until morning.
Wonder, what entreaties
the moth made to her?

aise vahshi kahaan hain ae khuubaan
Mir ko tum a'bas udaas kiya

The really crazy and the wild ones like me
are hard to find, O beautiful ones!
You disappointed Mir for no reason.

33

munh taka hi kare hai jis tis ka
hairati hai y aaiina kis ka

It looks at the face of each and every one.
With whose beauty the mirror is awestruck
as its eye is always open?

shaam se kuchh bujha sa rahta huun
dil hua hai charaagh muflis ka

When evening comes
my heart loses its verve.
It starts to quiver
like a poor man's lamp.

daagh aankhon se khil rahe hain sab
haath dasta hua hai nargis ka

The wounds are flowering
as open eyes.

The palm appears
like a bouquet of narcissus.

faiz ae abr chashm-e tar se utha
aaj daaman vas'ii hai us ka

O clouds, why don't you benefit
from the eyes holding tears?
Today, they are extremely generous.

taab kis ko jo haal-e Mir sune
haal hi aur kuchh hai majlis ka

Who has the patience
to hear the tragic story of Mir?
People in the assembly
have already lost their verve.

34

makke gaya madiine gaya karbala gaya
jaisa gaya tha vaisa hi chal phir ke aa gaya

He went to Makka and Madina.
He went to Karbla as well.
But he came back the same person—
as he was the day he left.

vo mujh se bhaagta hi phira kibr o naaz se
jon jon niyaaz kar ke main us se laga gaya

She always moved away from me
showing her pride and coquetry.
The more I desired her, closer I got to her,
more arrogance and vanity I found.

dekha jo raah jaate tabakhtur ke saath use
phir mujh shikasta-pa se n ik-dam raha gaya

When I saw her walking
showing vanity and conceit,
then the helpless me
could not simply resist.

baitha to boriye ke taiin sar p rakh ke Mir
saf kis adab se ham fuqara ki utha gaya

When I sat Mir
I used the same old sack
which I use as a pillow.
With what great abandon
and carefree manner
I acted as a dervish.

35

y Mir-e sitam kushta kisu waqt javaan tha
andaaz-e sukhan ka sabab shor o fughaan tha

This victim of circumstances named Mir
was once a young man.
His style of recitation of poetry
was filled with commotion and sadness.

jaadu ki pudi parcha-e abiyaat tha us ka
munh takiye ghazal parhte a'jab sehr biyaan tha

His notebook of verse
was like a little package of magic.
His face was worth looking at
as he recited his ghazal.
His style of recitation
was truly an act of wizardry!

jis raah se vo dil zadah dilli mein nikalta
saath us ke qayaamat ka sa hangaama ravaan tha

Whatever pathway in the city of Dilli
that man with an afflicted heart walked,
people always followed him and
he carried with him doomsday-like commotion.

afsurda n tha aisa k jon aab-zadah khaak
aandhi thi bala tha koi aashob jahaan tha

His melancholy persona
was not like moistened dust.
He was like a storm, a calamity,
an upheaval for the whole world.

kis martaba thi hasrat-e diidaar mere saath
jo phuul meri khaak se nikla nigraan tha

I carried within my heart
a great desire to see her;
the flower that sprouted from my grave
was in full glory and watchful.

go Mir jahaan mein kinhon ne tujh ko n jaana
maujuud n tha tu to kahaan naam o nishaan tha

Although Mir you did not get
the discerning attention that you deserved,
but do realize you were unfathomable,
not easy to be discovered and people
could not find you anywhere.

36

hamaare aage tera jab kisu ne naam liya
dil-e sitam zadah ko ham ne thaam thaam liya

When someone mentioned
your name in my presence,
I had to take hold
of my badly beaten heart.

kharaab rahte the masjid ke aage maikhaane
nigaah-e mast ne saaqi ki intiqaam liya

Mosques always looked upon taverns
as places of trouble.
But this in fact was the punishment
that intoxicated eyes of Saqi bestowed.

vo kaj ravish n mila raaste mein mujh se kabhi
n siidhi tarah se un ne mera salaam liya

The one who was vain and conceited
never crossed my path.
She did not even return my greetings
in a proper manner.

mere saliiqe se meri nibhi muhabbat mein
tamaam u'mr mein naakaamiyon se kaam liya

Thanks to my sophisticated manners,
I did well while I was in love,
though I faced one defeat after another
all my life.

agarche goṡha ġaziin huun main shaay'iron mein Mir
p mere shor ne ruue zamiin tamaam liya

Although in the company of poets,
I considered myself a humble person,
but whenever I spoke
my voice reverberated all across the globe.

37

jo kaho tum se baja hai saahib
ham bure hi sahi bhala saahib

Dear, what you say is perfectly correct.
I am so bad and that also is correct, Sahib.

saadah zahni mein nukta chiin the tum
ab to hain harf aashna saahib

In your naive days,
you were quite critical.
Now you have fallen in love
with the words, Sahib.

bandagi ek apni kya kam hai
aur kuchh tum se kahiye kya saahib

My unflinching devotion to you
is no less in any manner.
What more can I say, Sahib?

phir gaii-iin aankhein tum n aan phire
dekha tum ko bhi vaah vaah saahib

I kept waiting my whole life
and then my eyes closed,
but you never came.
I praised the Lord, Sahib.

kin ne sun she'r Mir y n kaha
kahiyo phir haae kya kaha saahib

Whosoever listened
to Mir recite his couplets
ever resist saying:
Please say it again, vaah!
What did you say, Sahib?

38

zakham jhele daagh bhi khaaye bahut
dil laga kar ham to pachhtaaye bahut

I suffered wounds
and I was the target
of many blemishes.
I fell in love,
but regretted it greatly.

dair se suu-e haram aaya n tuk
ham mizaaj apna idhar laaye bahut

From the idols I couldn't move
to the sacred sanctum even once,
although I tried my best.

phuul gul shams o qamar saare hi the
par hamein in mein tumhiin bhaaye bahut

There were buds and flowers.
There was the sun and the moon.
They all were available.
But, my luck, I liked you the most.

Mir se puuchha jo main aa'shiq ho tum
ho ke kuchh chupke se sharmaaye bahut

I asked Mir:
Are you a lover?
He fell silent
and felt self-effacing
and diffident.

39

amiiron tak rasaaii ho chuki bas
meri bakht aazmaaii ho chuki bas

Approached the rich—
that was it.
Tried my luck—
that was it.

bahaar ab ke bhi jo guzri qafas mein
to phir apni rahaaii ho chuki bas

Even this time
I spent the spring in a cell.
My freedom—
that was it.

n aaya vo mere jaate jahaan se
yahiin tak aashnaaii ho chuki bas

She didn't come to see me
as I left this world.
The limit of our love—
that was it.

laga hai hausla bhi karne tangi
ghamon ki ab samaaii ho chuki bas

Even my enthusiasm
seems impoverished.
Taken care of my sufferings—
that was it.

baraabar khaak ke to kar dikhaaya
falak bas be-adaaii ho chuki bas

You made me feel
like dust.
O God, enough is enough
my luck ran out—
that was it.

gale mein gervi kafni hai ab Mir
tumhaari mirzaaii ho chuki bas

Mir, you have around your neck a saffron shroud
similar to the one borne by vagabonds.
Your status as a Mirza—
that was it.

40

khush n aaii tumhaari chaal hamein
yuun n karna tha paiimaal hamein

I was not destined to have your love
But the way you trampled me under your foot,
it was too much!

haal kya puuchh puuchh jaate ho
kabhi paate bhi ho bahaal hamein

You come and inquire
about my wellbeing.
Do you ever find me
fully recovered?

kab tak is tangna mein khiinchi-ye ranj
yaan se yaarab tu hi nikaal hamein

How long can I suffer being a castaway like this?
O God, you are the only one who can save me
from this seclusion.

vajah kya hai k Mir munh p tere
nazar aata hai kuchh malaal hamein

What is the reason Mir
that I see on your face
traces of hidden sorrow and grief?

41

baare duniya mein raho gham-zadah ya shaad raho
aisa kuchh kar ke chalo yaan k bahut yaad raho

Live in the world—sad or happy.
But do something for which
people remember you
when you are no longer there.

ham ko diivaangi shahron hi mein khush aati hai
dasht mein qais raho koh mein farhaad raho

Madness works for me in the city.
Let Majnun be in the desert and
and Farhad in the mountains.

vo graan khwaab jo hai naaz ka apne so hai
daad be-daad raho shab ko k fariyaad raho

She is so conceited
and lost in her pride.

She cares even less—
be it lamentation in the night
or prayers during the day.

Mir ham mil ke bahut khush hue tum se pyaare
is kharaabe mein meri jaan tum aabaad raho

Mir, I was so very happy
to meet you, my dearest!
In this wily world
stay well, my life!

42

aage hamaare a'hd se vahshat ko ja n thi
divaangi kisu ki bhi zanjiir-e paa n thi

In the days gone by,
there was no place for my kind of frenzy.
Madness was not chained
around anybody's feet.

begaana sa lage hai chaman ab khizaan mein haae
aisi gaaii bahaar magar aashna n thi

The garden looks strange
this time of autumn, alas!
Spring left in a way
as if it never belonged here.

kab tha y shor-e nauha tera i'shq jab n tha
dil tha hamaara aage to maatam sara n thi

There was no sad song of death
when I was not in love with you.
I had full command over my heart and
it was not like a house of mourning.

vo aur koi ho gi saher jab hui qubuul
sharminda-e asar to hamaari du'aa n thi

It must be a different kind of morning
when the invocation was accepted.
My prayer, I know, had no effect at all.

aage bhi tere i'shq se khiinche the dard o ranj
lekin hamaari jaan par aisi bala n thi

It happened in the past too
when my heart was crushed
by pain and anguish in your love.
But it wasn't that bad a calamity
for my soul.

puzhmurdah is qadar hain k hai shub-h ham ko Mir
tan mein hamaare jaan kabhu thi bhi ya n thi

It is so withered that I doubt, Mir,
there ever was a time
when there was or wasn't
a sign of life in my body

43

kuchh karo fikr mujh diivaane ki
dhuum hai phir bahaar aane ki

Please do think
of someone afflicted like me.
Everyone is talking about
the incoming spring.

vo jo phirta hai mujh se duur hi duur
hai y taqriib ji ke jaane ki

I am talking about the one
who is avoiding me.
It is an indication to celebrate—
the loss of my heart.

tez yuun hi n thi shab-e aatish-e shauq
thi khabar garm us ke aane ki

There was a reason
for the fire of my passion
to be so intense.
There was news of
her impending visit.

kisu kam-zarf ne lagaaii aah
tujh se maikhaane ke jalaane ki

Some silly creature
has spread the news
that you of all people
set fire to the tavern.

jo hai so paaemaal-e gham hai Mir
chaal be-dol hai zamaane ki

Everything in this world
is ruined by sorrow, Mir.
It is unfair the way
time treats us all.

44

ho gaaii shahr shahr rusvaaii
ae meri maut tu bhali aaii

My name was defamed
in city after city.
O my death!
You caused all this.

yak bayaabaan b-rang-e saut-e jaras
mujh p hai bekasi o tanhaaii

Just like the forlorn
sounds of bells in a desert,
I am overcome
by helplessness and loneliness.

sar rakhuun us ke paaon par lekin
dast-e qudrat y main kahaan paaii

I can place my head on her feet
but fate has not given me
the capacity to do all this.

Mir jab se gaya hai dil tab se
main to kuchh ho gaya huun saudaaii

Mir, since the day
I gave away my heart,
I am showing signs
of losing my mind.

45

jin jin ko tha y i'shq ka aazaar mar gaye
aksar hamaare saath ke biimaar mar gaye

Those who suffered from the malady of love,
they all passed away.
Most of the afflicted ones were my buddies;
they too passed away.

sad karvaan vafa hai koi puuchhta nahien
goya mat'a-e dil ke kharidaar mar gaye

There are caravans of constant love,
no one cares.
It appears all those who wanted to buy
a precious commodity called heart—
they too passed away.

majnun n dasht mein hai n farhaad koh mein
tha jin se lutf-e zindagi ve yaar mar gaye

There is no Majnun in the desert
and no Farhad in the mountains.
All those who were the source
of joy in my life,
they have all passed away.

46

ghalib k y dil-khasta shab-e hijr mein mar jaaye
y raat nahien vo jo kahaani mein guzar jaaye

It is possible that the person
with a broken heart might die
in this night of separation.
This is not the night
that we can spend
telling stories.

ne but-kadah hai manzil-e maqsuud n kaa'ba
jo koi talaashi ho tera aah kidhar jaaye

Our destination is neither the temple
nor the sacred sanctum.
If there is anyone trying to find you,
where should one go?

har sub-h to khurshiid tere munh p charahe hai
aisa n ho y saada kahien ji mein utar jaaye

Each morning
the sun illuminates your face.
I'm afraid that one day
it might just become you.

yaaquut koi in ko kahe hai koi gul-barg
tuk honth hila tu bhi k ik baat thahar jaaye

Some call them a ruby,
others call them a rose petal.
You need to say something
so that this matter is settled.

mat baith bahut i'shq ke aazurdah dilon mein
naala kisu mazluum ka taasiir n kar jaaye

You shouldn't sit in the company
of distressed ones.
The moans of an oppressed person
might make your worries come true.

47

ham huye tum huye k Mir hue
us ki zulfon ke sab asiir hue

Whether it is you or I
or simply Mir,
we are all prisoners
of her tresses.

nahien aate kisu ki aankhon mein
ho ke aa'shiq bahut haqiir hue

No one considers me
of any worth.
By falling in love
I fell into the ranks
of the worthless.

aage y be-adaaiiyaan kab thiin
in dinon tum bahut shariir hue

Never in the past
you were so playful.
These days, you have become
mischievous and alluring.

yaa'ni maanind-e sub-h duniya mein
ham jo paida hue so piir hue

Like dawn spreads its shine in the world,
I came-of-age when I was born.

48

kab se nazar lagi thi darvaaza-e haram se
pardah utha to lariyaan aankhein hamaari ham se

My eyes were fixated
on the door to the sanctum
for a long time.
When the veil was lifted,
my eyes saw me.

hasti mein ham ne aa kar aasuudgi n dekhi
khultiin n kaash aankhein khwaab-e khush-e a'dam se

I found no contentment
by being in the world.
I wish my eyes had not opened
from the dream of non-being.

paamaal kar ke ham ko pachhtaao ge bahut tum
kamyaab hain jahaan mein sar dene vale ham se

My ruin
you will regret a lot.
People like me
who are ready to offer
their heads for love
are rare in this world.

dil do ho Mir saahib us badma'aash ko tum
khaatir to jam'a kar lo tuk qol se qasam se

You are giving away
your heart
to a cheat, Mir Sahib.
Make a calculation,
please take an oath
or a pledge.

49

gham raha jab tak k dam mein dam raha
dil ke jaane ka nihaayat gham raha

I remained in the grip of grief
as long as I lived.
I was particularly agonized
by the loss of my heart.

sunte hain laila ke khaime ko siyaah
us mein majnun ka magar maatam raha

We hear that Laila lived
in a black tent.
But inside,
there was mourning
for Majnun.

mere rone ki haqiiqat jis mein thi
ek muddat tak vo kaaghaz nam raha

Something that contained the secret
of my crying,
for a long time that piece of paper
remained moist.

50

shahron mulkon mein jo y Mir kahaata hai miyaan
diidni hai p bahut kam nazar aata hai miyaan

In the cities and in the countries
this man who is known as Mir
is worth seeing,
but he is not easy to find, Miyan.

aa'lam aaiina hai jis ka vo musavvir be-misl
haae kya suurtein parde mein banaata hai miyaan

The one who holds a mirror to the world
is an artist without a comparison.
What beautiful faces He paints on the canvas, Miyan!

qismat is bazm mein laaii k jahaan ka saaqi
de hai mai sab ko hamein zahr pilaata hai miyaan

My luck is such I have been brought
into an assembly whose Saqi

serves wine to all but me.
She offers me nothing but poison, Miyan.

ho ke aa'shiq tere jaan o dil o diin kho baithe
jaisa karta hai koi vaisa hi paata hai miyaan

I lost my heart and soul
after I fell in love with you.
True! As you sow,
so shall you reap, Miyan!

husn yak chiiz hai ham hovein k tu ho naaseh
aisi shai se koi bhi haath uthaata hai miyaan

Beauty is a thing of such wonder
it attracts one and all,
be it you, me, or the austere priest.
Who will take away his hand
from such an object, Miyan?

kya pari-khwaan hai jo raaton ko jaga de hai Mir
shaam se dil jigar o jaan jalaata hai miyaan

What a magician who can call fairies
and make the nights glow, Mir.
As evening descends,
he burns heart and soul
all with such a yearning, Miyan.

Part II

The Beauty of Mir's Poetic Voice*

*   Part II of the book is based on Gopi Chand Narang's *Usloobiyaat-e Meer* (Delhi: Educational Publishing House, 2013, fourth printing).

A Poet of Countless Delights

lutf mujh mein bhi hain hazaaron Mir
diidni huun jo soch kar dekho

I am filled with countless delights, Mir.
I am worth a look if you observe me,
as thoughtfully as you can.

In *Tazkirah-e Khush Ma'rika-e Zeba* written by Saa'dat Khan
Nasir Lakhnavi (circa 1845), there is a description of an
interesting episode involving Mir Taqi Mir and an elderly,
much respected poet, Mirza Rafi Sauda. The incident took place
at the residence of Sirajuddin Khane Arzu, a great scholar, who
was the maternal uncle of Mir's stepbrother, and at whose
place in Delhi Mir was temporarily staying, receiving his initial
training from him. Arzu told the young Mir that Sauda had
visited in the morning and had read the following *matl'a* (first
couplet of a ghazal) with the pride of an established poet:

chaman mein sub-h jo us jangju ka naam liya
saba ne tegh ka aab-e ravaan se kaam liya

This morning while I was in the garden,
I alluded to the name of my killer-beloved.
The playful breeze got a hint and turned
the shimmering water that was in motion into a lancet.

Mir listened to the couplet carefully and then spontaneously recited the following couplet, which he composed in the moment:

hamaare aage tera jab kisu ne naam liya
dil-e sitam zada ko apne thaam thaam liya

When someone mentioned
your name in my presence,
I had a hard time controlling myself and
I put my hand on the wounded heart.

Khane Arzu was visibly pleased and uttered the traditional invocation: 'May God save you from an evil eye!'[1] This ghazal of seven couplets is found in Mir's first Divan. He later corrected the second line—to *dil-e sitam zada ko ham ne thaam thaam liya*—making it rhythmically more appealing. Maulana Hali in his book *Muqaddama-e Sh'er o Shaa'yiri* especially commented on this couplet while critiquing Mir's poetry. He wrote: 'Only those poets can infuse their passion in such subtle words who know how to use a harmless knife to do the work of a sharp lancet.

---

[1] Saa'dat Khan Nasir Lakhnavi, Shamim Inhonavi, ed. *Tazkirah-e Khush Ma'rka Zeba* (Lucknow: Nasim Book Depot, 1971).

And only people with fine creative taste can fathom the depth of such passion.'[2]

Although Mir's father was greatly respected and had many followers, they became indifferent to the family when the father left behind unpaid debt. By leaving Agra, the place of his birth, Mir tried to make a new start with his life. But there were hurdles and disappointment at every step of the way. The stay at Khane Arzu's house was short-lived because his stepbrother wrote a nasty letter to his uncle suggesting that he should not help Mir because he was a 'troublesome person'. Khane Arzu's behaviour changed overnight towards Mir. The treatment that the so-called 'uncle' meted out to Mir was worse than that of an enemy. Mir separated himself from Khane Arzu and learned to live in a city that was frequently under attack by invaders and hounded by calamities.

There was an age difference of about ten years between Sauda (1713–80) and Mir (1722–1810). By the time Mir started his poetic quest, Sauda was at the height of his popularity. Mir lived longer, and as the years went by, Mir's poetry came to be known for its heart-warming quality. His words which had a compassionate flair won critical acclaim. But, unfortunately, all his life, Sauda's fame cast a shadow over Mir due to his popularity with nobles and nawabs as well as the literati of the time. Several commentators, notably Mus-hafi, Mirza Ali Lutf, and Mustafa Khan Shefta, who wrote *Tazkirahs* of Urdu poets during the eighteenth century tended to place the two

---

[2]   Altaf Hussain Hali, *Muqaddma-e She'r o Shaa'yiri* (New Delhi: Maktaba Jamia, 2013).

poets in the same pigeonhole. Notice the following apologetic assessment by Mus-hafi from his *Tazkirah-e Hindi*: 'Many compare the two and comment that maybe Mir has an edge in masnavi and ghazal, but in qasida[3] and *hajv* (satire) Sauda is by far the best.'[4] Mirza Ali Lutf writes in his *Gulshan-e Hind*: 'The truth is that Mir has attained a distinctive place for himself in ghazal, but in qasidah and masnavi Rafi Sauda has no equal.'[5] Shefta went further and in the style of an adage wrote about Mir in his *Gulshan-e Be-khaar*: 'His high is too high and low is too low.'[6] This adage, a sharp tongue-in-cheek compliment, later became a public quote to downgrade Mir's poetic contribution. This type of proverbial generalizations were a gross injustice to a master poet's multidimensional, layered, and inventive oeuvre, as we would demonstrate in our analysis.

Hallmark of a Distinctive Creativity

agarche gosha nashiin huun main shaa'yiron mein Mir
p mere shor ne ruue zamiin tamaam kya

Although I quietly sit
in a lonely corner
in the galaxy of poets,

---

[3] At that time, qasida was considered a superior and a master genre.

[4] Ghulam Hamdani Mus-hafi, Maulvi Abdul Haq ed. *Tazkirah-e Hindi* (Delhi: Jaam'e Barqi Press, 1933).

[5] Mirza Ali Lutf, Ata Kakovi ed. *Gulshan-e Hind* (n.p.: Azeem Alshaan Book Depot, 1972).

[6] Mustafa Khan Shefta, *Tazkirah Gulshan-e Be-khaar* (Lucknow: Nawal Kishore, 1874).

but my lyrical voice
has conquered the world.

The above couplet makes it clear that right from the beginning Mir had a feeling that he was different from other poets. His creativity was such that even in his younger years he was writing couplets that were distinctive. This distinguishing characteristic became his hallmark in later years. Sauda's couplet that we read above was nothing ordinary. It had all the markings of rhetorical and crafty poetry. But it doesn't touch the reader's heart in the same way as Mir's couplet. What is the secret? A good couplet has a mix of inventive meaning, free flow, and a heart luring quality. The presence of such elements and mellowness separate Mir's couplet from that of Sauda. As a first step, it is worth noting that Sauda's couplet contains a medley of nouns such as *chaman, sub-h, jangju, saba, tegh, aab, kaam*—seven in all. Mir has just one noun—*dil-e sitam zada*—around which the whole couplet is built. The effortless verbal structure used by Mir was far ahead of his time, unique among his contemporaries, and a primary reason for the genial and affable sweetness of his verse that left arty and lofty poets like Sauda far behind. Syed Abdullah has mentioned a couplet by one of Sauda's disciples where he wonders how a poet who wrote in the common colloquial language could surpass a poet like Sauda who wrote in the rhetorical modes established by the great Persian masters like Naziri and Zahuri.[7] Here is his couplet:

---

[7]   Syed Abdullah, *Naqd-e Mir* (Lahore: Aaina-e Adab,1958).

jo aisi zabaan mein ho ghazal us ko kahien bad
aur lehje mein ho aa'm ke so paaye vo tauqiir

Isn't it strange that a ghazal
written in an ornate language
is labeled worthless?
And the one in ordinary speech
gets all the respect?

The term commonplace or ordinary speech, often used for
Mir's verse, was the principal misleading factor. We would
address it later. The vital point here is that Mir's simplicity is
deceptive, and it deceived the critics for centuries. This idea
was so widespread that even Mir's metaphorical caveat was
not taken note of for quite some time.

koi saadah hi us ko saadah kahe
hamein to lage hai vo a'iyaar sa

Only a simpleton would call him simple.
To me he looks like an ingenious sorcerer.

Mir makes this assertion time and again. Using conversational
language does not make his verse simple. We will unfold this
deception step by step.

Poetic Attributes of Rekhta

rekhta rutbe ko pahunchaaya hua us ka hai
mo'taqid kaun nahien Mir ki ustaadi ka

If Rekhta reached the pinnacle of its greatness,
this was the work that he accomplished.
Is there anyone who does not accept
Mir's masterly and mysterious touch?

Mir has mentioned, and he agreed with Qayem Chandpuri
in this, that his *maa'shuuq* (the raw idiom that inspired
him) was a resident of Dakan—a veiled reference to Wali's
Dakani poetry. We should not forget that at the time when
Mir was writing, Urdu was still raw and at best a work in
progress. Mir was not only using an imperfect language; he
was also creatively perfecting it through the process of his
poetic weaving.

In his *Tazkirah Nikaat-us Sho'ra* Mir mentions six
categories of Rekhta. First, there was a practice inspired by
Amir Khusrau, of using Persian for the first line and Hindavi
for the second. For example:

yaka yak az dil do chashm-e jaadu basad farebum b burd taskiin
kise pari hai k ja sunaave pyaare pi ko hamaari batiyaan

Like a flash of lightening
those two eyes pierced my heart.
I wish someone were there
to carry my message to my lover
on how hard I was hit.

Second, some poets used half a line of verse in Persian
and the other half in Hindavi or Hindi. Third, there was a
trend to create a poetic line that had all the verbal features

of Persian. Mir called such practices absurd. Fourth, only those usages and phrases which were in conformity with the linguistic genius of Rekhta are used. Mir wrote: 'But only a sensitive and creative mind could make this judgement. In the same manner, what is unsuitable and not in conformity with the genius of the soil should be discarded, again based on the poet's creative judgement. I am all for it and this is what I try to practice.' The fifth type was called *iihaam*—to use a word having double meanings, a sort of pun. It was quite prevalent at that time. This led to trite poetry, not written for creativity but for jugglery or play of words. Mir rejected this type. 'I am not in favour of it and cannot recommend it.' The sixth kind uses all standard devices for beautification like *fasaahat, balaaghat, tajniis, ada-bandi, khayaal, etc.*[8] which the masters had perfected over centuries. Mir liked their artfulness for writing inventive poetry and he praised this type.

The sixth category combined with the fourth is what Mir preferred; and he called this distinctive, synthesized, and chiselled style as his *andaaz* (style).[9]

It is unfortunate that most of the literary criticism of the time simply ignored what Mir had stated about his unique creative poetic style. He was generally referred to as Khudaa-e Sukhan, meaning the God of Poesy, but no one cared to

---

[8]   These are culture specific terms and the nearest meaning could be: clarity, flow, lyricism, mellowness; artfulness, depth and ingenuity of meaning; alliteration, musicality of words; intricate finesse; thoughtfulness and developing linkages of themes.

[9]   Mir Taqi Mir, Maulvi Abdul Haq ed, *Nikaat-us Sho'ra* (Karachi: Anjuman Taraqqi Urdu Pakistan, 1935, 1979 reprint).

elaborate why he deserved to be called the best of the best, and what were the distinctive features of his golden voice, his andaaz.

After Mohammad Husain Azad, who wrote about Mir in the nineteenth century, Maulavi Abdul Haq was the first to publish Mir's poetic selection in the early twentieth century together with a detailed critical appreciation. But his common refrain was Mir's simplicity. Jafar Ali Khan Asar Lakhnavi, who was a great admirer of Mir, also presented a good analysis, but his examination too lacked any critical insight. Even when he tried hard, the only thing he said was that there is an unusual flow in Mir's work, there is sweep and gush, pain and suffering, and these distinctive elements can be appreciated by sophisticated minds. All this is fine, but there is much more to Mir than that. A quick assessment does not complete the picture. Mir was the first great Indian poet who used multiple lenses in his work. His deceptive simplicity was in fact his 'multiplicity'. Both Ghalib and Iqbal are great poets, but they too borrow many phrases and features perfected by Mir as part of his andaaz. There are multiple streams coming from different traditions that merge and amalgamate into Mir's verse and this results in a creative confluence that has not been seen in any other poet. There is a strong link between Iqbal and Ghalib and between Ghalib and Mir with respect to what Ghalib called Bedil's 'spring-like creativity'. Both Maulvi Abdul Haq and Syed Abdullah rightly say that Ghalib's poetic style has its roots in Mir, whose poetry has several treasures of meaning (*ganjiina-e maa'ni*) that Ghalib took to greater heights.

Fundamental Stylistic Attributes

gali mein us ki gaya so gaya n bola phir
main Mir Mir kar us ko bahut pukar raha

I went to her lane.
It did happen.
Didn't say a word after.
I called Mir, Mir—
an echo of silence,
no response!

While interpreting Mir's work, we should keep in mind that we can't make any judgement based on examples that are similar in essence. Any such attempt will be incomplete. Mir can't be understood at the surface level. This is the weakness of logical reasoning—everything happens in a 'serial' fashion. But stylistic distinctions are rarely arranged as a sequence that eventually form a construction. They appear as one layer that sits upon another in a synthesized manner. There is always some difficulty in separating one layer from another. Let us look at a famous ghazal by Mir followed by two couplets of a ghazal by Ghalib and we shall examine their similarities and differences.

ulti ho gaein sab tadbiirein kuchh n dava ne kaam kiya
dekha is biimaariye dil ne aakhir kaam tamaam kiya

All my plans have collapsed,
and medicines have no effect.

This heart's sickness
has brought life to its end.

a'hd-e javaani ro ro kaata piiri mein lein aankhein muund
y'aani raat bahut the jaage sub-h hui aaraam kiya

There was lot of weeping and crying during my youth,
and in old age I closed my eyes.
It was like there was lot of sleeplessness during the night,
but when the dawn broke, my sleep returned, and I rested.

harf nahien jaan-bakhshi mein us ki khuubi apni qismat ki
ham se jo pehle keh bheja so marne ka paighaam kiya

I do not question her power to grant me life,
but there is something peculiar with my luck.
The first message that I received from her
was ironically a death sentence.

naa-haq ham majbuuron par y tohmat hai mukhtaari ki
chaahte hain so aap karein hain ham ko a'bas badnaam kiya

The powerless are said to possess a free will.
It is nothing more than slander.
Actually, what He wills happens,
but we get blamed without any reason.

kis ka kaa'ba kaisa qibla kaun haram hai kiya ahraam
kuuche ke us ke baashindon ne sab ko yahiin se salaam kiya

Who is looking for Kaba, or direction for one's prayer?
Or the robes to be worn on holy pilgrimage?
People of this city of non-conformists offer their greetings
while sitting here and without going anywhere.

sheikh jo hai masjid mein nanga raat ko tha maikhaane mein
hubba kharqa kurta topi masti mein in'aam kiya

Sheikh, who spent the night in the tavern,
stands naked in the mosque.
And in his drunken state, he gave away
his cloak, his gown, his shirt, and his cap.

yaan ke saped o siyaah mein ham ko dakhl jo hai so itna hai
raat ko ro ro sub-h kiya ya din ko jon ton shaam kiya

I have little say or control
in the black and white ways of this world.
I spend the night crying and spend the day
waiting for the evening to arrive.

sub-h chaman mein us ko kahien takliif-e hava le aaii thi
rukh se gul ko mol liya qaamat se sarv ghulaam kiya

She wanted fresh air,
so she walked into the garden in the morning.
She subdued the rose with her rosy cheeks,
and with her tall figure, she made the cypress her slave.

saa'd-e siimiin donon us ke haath mein laa kar chhor diye
bhuule us ke qaul o qasam par haae khayaal-e khaam kiya

I held her tender silver wrists in my hands
and then let them go. What stupidity!
She wasted no time in forgetting
the promises and vows she made.

aise aahuue ram khurdah ki vahshat khoni mushkil thi
sehr kiya ai'jaaz kiya jin logon ne tujh ko raam kiya

It was difficult to tame
the wild and beautiful one
with gazelle-like eyes.
Those who succeeded
may have used, I wonder,
some magic or miracle.

Mir ke diin o mazhab ko ab puuchhte kiya ho un ne to
qashqa khaincha dair me baitha kab ka tark islaam kiya

Why do you ask Mir's religion?
Or what he believes in?
He put a sandal mark on his forehead
and he was found sitting in a temple.
He gave up on Islam a long time ago.

Mirza Ghalib wrote a ghazal of five couplets in the same *zamiin* (a lyrical invention with a rhyming scheme and musicality). Two couplets of the ghazal, the matl'a and the *maqt'a* (the last couplet) are presented below for comparison. It may be mentioned that Ghalib's ghazal was found in *Nuskha-e Bhopal,* a collection that included ghazals written during 1813–16. This places Ghalib's age,

when he wrote the ghazal, between sixteen to nineteen
years.

vahshi ban sayyaad ne ham ram khurdon ko kya raam kia
rishta-e chaak-e jeb-e daridah sarf-e qimaash-e daam kiya

Lovers became wild huntsmen
to subdue their untamable beloveds.
It doesn't matter if clothes were torn
and what was left had to be sold off.

shaam-e firaaq-e yaar mein josh-e khiira-sari se ham ne Asad
maah ko dar tasbiih-e kavaakib jaaye nashiin-e imam kiya

During the night of separation
and in our passionate insanity, Asad,
I turned the stars into a rosary
with 101st bead looking like moon—
a symbol for the missed cherished one.

Mir's ghazal is from his early collection and it is included in
his first Divan. It has a total of fifteen couplets of which eleven
were selected and translated above. As stated above, Ghalib's
ghazal was also from his early years. While comparing the two
ghazals, Syed Abdullah writes: 'In these two ghazals, leaving
aside one couplet or so, there is very little similarity when
we look at the subject matter and the style of presentation.
It seems that Ghalib entered the fray with a lot of force and
excitement, but he could not compete with the vast array of
Mir's *qaafiya*s (rhyming scheme). He ended the ghazal after

writing only five couplets. Compared with Mir's wholesome and very effective and free-flowing presentation, Ghalib's verse appears to be a collection of colourful words. Yet it is true that we feel a commotion demonstrating the poet's search for a higher ground.'[10]

First, let's do a quick analysis of signifying elements. There is no doubt that these two ghazals are representative of two different poetic voices. In Ghalib's matl'a there are nine nouns and adjectives: *vahshi, sayyaad, ram khurda, rishta, chaak, jeb, daridaah, qimaash*, and *daam*. What do we find in Mir's matl'a? In the first line, there is *dava* and in the second there is *biimariye dil*. The entire couplet has three nouns and three verbal nodes.

The second point relates to the fact that Mir uses long *bahr* (lyrical meter) with small grammatical units that work as nodes of meaning, points where several lines and pathways intersect, and have spontaneity in expressing emotions. Third, Mir uses fewer nouns and therefore he is less in need of *izafat*s.[11] Ghalib uses five izafats in the second line of his matl'a which makes it tough to read and too dense in its meaning. Fourth, Mir's modes of expression have deep roots with the soil that he shows in his indigenous touch. In Ghalib's ghazal there are no retroflex voices, which are typically Prakritik. It is not that these voices are missing in all of Ghalib, but he uses them sparingly. For Mir, retroflex comes naturally because he draws inspiration from the spoken language that is filled with

---

[10] Abdullah, *Naqd-e Mir,* p. 281.

[11] *Izafat* is a connection between two words (compounded word). It is indicated as -e. It can be adjectival, otherwise it stands for possessive *ka, ke, ki.*

close to the soil idiomatic expressions that was neither formal nor literary.

Last, Mir is rather fond of using vowels, especially long vowels, which help in creating a racy flow as opposed to dense formulations. Let us look at the following examples. The signifying verbal or vocative nodes which flow effortlessly and communicate instantaneously are shown with slashes. Needless to say, this is a hallmark of Mir's distinctive creativity.

dil ki tah ki kahi nahien jaati / naazuk hai asraar bahut
anchhar to hain i'shq ke do hi / lekin hai bistaar bahut

I can't describe the depth of my heart.
It is delicate and secretive.
Love's magic is limited to one or two,
but its spread is immensely mysterious.

milne lage ho der der / dekhiye/ kya hai kya nahien
tum to karo ho saahibi / bande mein kuchh raha nahien

Meeting me after a long spell!
Let us see how it goes.
What is and what is not.
You act like a sovereign.
But there is nothing left
in the humble me.

kin niindon ab tu soti hai / ai chashm-e girya naak
mizhgaan to khol / shahr ko sailab le gaya

What kind of sleep are you having?
Open your tear-filled eyes.
The flood has swept away the city!

dil baham pahuncha badan mein / tap se sara tan jala
aa pari y aisi chingaari / k pairaahan jala

My heart felt the body.
With fever it burnt.
It was quite a spark!
O gosh, it has burnt everything
my whole self!

khuub hai ae abr / yak shab aao / baaham roiiye
par n itna bhi k duube shahr / kam kam roiiye

It is great, O cloud,
that you show up one evening!
We can cry together.
But not so much
that we drown the city.
We cry but not that much.

shahr-e dil aah a'jab jaaye thi / par us ke gaye
aisa ujra / k kisi tarah basaaya n gaya

Heart's city was an enchanting place.
But when she left, it was ruined.
It never got its liveliness back.

kya jaaniye / k chhaati jale hai k daagh-e dil
ik aag si lagi hai / kahien kuchh dhuuaan sa hai

I don't know
whether the chest is on fire
or the wounds of my heart.
There is some smoke around.

ab ke bahut hai shor-e bahaaraan / ham ko mat zanjiir karo
dil ki havas tuk ham bhi nikaalein / dhuumein ham ko machaane do

The spring has arrived
with a lot of tumult.
Don't chain me please.
Let me fill my heart's desire
and cause some commotion.

kahta tha kisu se kuchh / takta tha kisu ka munh
kal Mir khara tha yaan / sach hai / k diivaana tha

He was saying something to someone.
He was looking awestruck at someone.
Yesterday, Mir was standing here.
It is true. He had lost his mind.

Here are some verses from a ghazal that show creative use of racy long vowels, multiple nodes and an extreme form of spontaneity that spurs lyricism.

aa'lam aa'lam i'shq o junuun hai / duniya duniya tohmat hai
dariya dariya rota huun main / sahra sahra vahshat hai

The world is filled with love and reckless passion,
The whole thing looks like someone's imagination.
When I cry, it seems rivers are flowing.
There is nothing but gay abandon and wildness.

koi dam raunaq majlis ki / aur bhi hai is dam ke saath
yaa'ni charaagh sub-h ke hain ham / dam apna bhi ghaniimat hai

The splendour of her gathering
lasts as long as the breath.
I am like a night lamp.
Few breaths, and the night is gone.

khaak se aadam kar ke uthaaya / jis ko dast-e qudrat ne
qadar nahien kuchh us bande ki / y bhi khuda ki qudrat hai

He lifted a pile of dust and cast Adam with His hands.
He gave him a form and the gift of life.
But the same human being has no worth today.
This too is the will of God!

sub-h se aansu na-umiidaana / jaise vidaaii aata tha
aaj kisu khwaahish ki shaayad / dil se hamaare rukhsat hai

Tears have been flowing
since this morning.
Am I saying farewell?
If there was a deep desire,
tragically it is leaving for good!

kya dilkash hai bazm jahaan ki / jaate yaan se jise dekho
vo gham diidah ranj kashiidah / aah saraapa hasrat hai

This worldly gathering—
it is filled with attractions.
You know this when you see
someone leaving this world.
Unhappy, filled with grief,
carrying unfulfilled desires.

Last Master of the Oral Tradition

parhte phirein ge galiyon mein in rekhton ko log
muddat rahein gi yaad y baatein hamaariyaan

The people will keep singing these verses
going through the streets and surroundings.
What I have said will keep echoing forever.

Mir lived and wrote nearly two and a half centuries ago. During the last phase of his life, the printing press had become a reality. Mir's *Kulliyaat* was printed and published by the Fort Williams College in 1811, but unfortunately Mir passed away a year earlier in 1810. Therefore, he never saw a printed copy of his Divan. How the printing press impacted creative styles of Urdu literature and poetry has not been fully analysed or understood. Up to that time, the literary tradition was basically an oral tradition. Slowly the oral practices were transformed into printed words—impressions in black on white paper bound as a book for reading. More than anything else, works of prose (*daastaan*s, which were tales and mythologies) gained popularity later during the nineteenth century and they reached a large number of readers. From this point of view, it appears that Mir was the last messenger of the oral tradition. He was very conscious of the fact that the magic of his poetry lay in verbal transmission from one person to another. *Aab-e Hayaat,* authored by Mohammad Husain Azad, considered to be Urdu poetry's first literary text, says that the purity of Mir's verse was sustained by his conversational style.[12] Syed Abdullah agreed that Mir was fully committed to his dialogic style. For example, let us take a closer look at the following couplets. Note the word, *baat, baatein,* oral speech, tale, and communication. He was conscious of the fact that his speaking voice was for the listener and not the reader of a book. The fact cannot be ignored that the oral tradition too was a trigger for his fluency and communicability.

baatein hamaari yaad rahein phir baatein n aisi suniye ga
parhte kisi ko suniye ga to der talak sar dhuniye ga

Remember the words that I speak
you will not hear anyone else speak like this.
If you listen to it again at all,
you will be truly moved by its enchantment.

baa'd hamaare is fan ka jo koi maahir hove ga
dard angez andaaz ki baatein aksar parh parh rovey ga

---

[12] Mohammad Hussain Azad, *Aab-e Hayaat* (Lahore: Malik Azad Book Depot, n.d.)

Whoever masters this art after I am gone
will find these tales highly heart-rending
and agonizing and then he too will be
deeply enthused like me!

Mir often uses *tum* or *tu* for informal speech instead of *aap,* or
words like *miyaan, pyaare, arey, saahib,* etc. When he addresses
himself, he typically uses honorifics like *Mir saahib* or *Mir ji.*
The following couplets demonstrate his addressing style.

lete hi naam us ka sote se chonk uthe ho
hai khair Mir saahib kuchh tum ne khwaab dekha

After uttering her name,
he suddenly woke up from his sleep.
Are you okay Mir Sahib?
Did you see a dream?

ji mein tha us se miliye to kya kya n kahiye Mir
par jab mile to rah gaye naachaar dekh kar

I knew it within my heart, Mir,
what to say to her.
But when I saw her,
I was rendered speechless.

chala n uth ke vahiin chupke chupke phir tu Mir
abhi to us ki gali se pukaar laaya huun

Mir, you sneaked into her lane
once again without making a rustle.

My God! Just a while ago I pulled you back
from there calling Mir, Mir!

pyaar karne ka jo khuubaan ham p rakhte hain gunaah
un se bhi to puuchhte tum itne pyaare kiyon huye

Those who tell me of committing a sin
for loving her should at least ask her
why she is so enchanting
and inexplicably seductive!

maqduur tak to zabt karuun huun p kya karuun
munh se nikal hi jaati hai ik baat pyaar ki

I try as far as I can
to restrain myself,
but a word of love
escapes one's lips
on its own.

sair ki ham ne har kahien pyaare
phir jo dekha to kuchh nahien pyaare

My loved one, I took a walk around
the whole world, up and down.
But then, my dear, I had a feeling
that there is nothing like you
anywhere in the world.

kya raftagi se meri tum guftagu karo ho
khoya gaya nahien main aisa jo koi paave

Will you have a dialogue
with my unconscious self?
I am certainly not lost in such a way
that anybody can find me.

kahte to ho yuun kahte yuun kahte jo vo aata
sab kahne ki baatein hain kuchh bhi n kaha jaata

Now you think what you should have said
when she came. This is empty talk.
When she really came, you were so lost—
you were not able to utter a word.

jab se javaan hue ho y chaal kya nikaali
jab tum chala karo ho thokar laga kare hai

Have you thought
about your stride
since you have bloomed?
When you walk,
you really hit my heart.

nahien hai chaah bhali itni bhi dua kar Mir
k ab jo dekhuun use main bahut n pyaar aave

So much love is not good for you, Mir.
Better pray for yourself.
You don't want to be overwhelmed
when you look at her endearingly.

Mir was essentially a poet of sharing and listening. Often, he compared his verse to telling a story or a *raam-kahaani*.[13]

fursat-e khwaab nahien zikr-e butaan mein ham ko
raat din raam-kahaani si suna karte hain

I don't have time for a dream
as I talk about that beautiful idol.
This is such an enticing story of my love
that Mir keeps repeating, day and night!

sar-guzasht apni kis andoh se shab kahta tha
so gaye tum n suni aah kahaani us ki

With what pain last night
Mir was telling his tale of love.
Ah, how sad, you did not hear
his traumatic tale and went to sleep!

A River Roaring and Gushing

turfa sanaa' hain ae Mir y mauzon tab'aan
baat jaati hai bigar to bhi bana dete hain

What an over-flowing poet Mir is!
A wonderful creativity on display!
Even if something goes wrong,
he fixes it right away and moves on.

---

[13] A reference to Hindu epic poem Ramayana.

When we talk about Mir, the conversation straightaway moves to his easy and fluent style and the simplicity of his verse. Even Ghalib mentioned this in one of his letters. But in reality, it is not something easy to put into practice. We know that metrical poetry has its own limitations. The poet has to work within a set of constraints. But Mir's artistry lies in the fact that even if the theme is intricate or thought is complex, with his wizard like creativity, he successfully delivers free-flowing verse while maintaining the basic structures of common spoken speech. Words seem to be like kneaded clay on a potter's spinning wheel and he is able to mould and shape them in any way he likes. In the couplets given below, Mir uses simple speaking nodes. If the first line of a couplet contains a statement and the second line provides a justification for that statement, then a couplet ordinarily has one or two nodes. But in Mir's poetry we find three, four or even more nodes in one couplet. Maulvi Abdul Haq admitted that Mir's poetry is effortless and fluent, yet it was not easy to specifically point out the secret of its distinctive qualities.

There is an interesting account in *Tazkirah-e Khush Ma'reka-e Zeba* that when Mir was young and passionate, he engaged in the poetry of name-calling. In those days, it was common to attack others and engage in the gamesmanship of notoriety, disgrace, scandal, blame, and condemnation. Khane Arzu once mentioned that disapprobation of loved ones is better than good vibes from undesirable others. The words used for an insulting outburst were transformed into creative expression in another context. One can feel a hidden surge and bitterness in Mir which indicates there is some truth to the account. Mir exhibited strong feelings and strong beliefs coupled with gushing creative ability. We cannot deny the fact that there is a strong relationship between passion and creativity. Inner commotion often leads to outer turmoil. Let us look at some of effusive and rapturous metaphoric expressions used by him.

lahu mein nahaana (bathing in blood)
khuun mein haath rangna (dipping your hands in blood)
aansuuon ka sailaab (the flood of tears)
aa'shiq ka baguula (the flaming of a lover)
dhuuaan ya ghuubaar ban-na (disappearing in a cloud of smoke)
saayaa-e divaar mein baithna (sitting in the shade of an enclosure wall)
dil ke ujre nagar mein akele charaagh ka jalna (sole lamp burning in the heart's desolate dwelling)
dhuaan sa hai kuchh us nagar ki taraf hona (burning smoke of a distant human habitat)
dhuuein ka dil o jaan se uthhna (smoke to rise from burning heart or self)
ustakhwaan kaanmp kaanmp jalna (the bones to crack and burn)
khaak se phuul ban kar namudaar hona (arising from the dust as a fresh flower)

The notion that Mir is a poet of seventy-two lancets is an unfair judgment. The statement, that some ascribe to Shefta, became famous giving rise to the impression that there is nothing more to Mir beyond the count of seventy-two so called lancet couplets. In fact, this claim was a misrepresentation of what Sadar-uddin Azurdah had stated: 'Mir's bad couplets are bad, but his best are beyond excellence.'

Mir often spoke of an uncontrollable gush and surge in his verse. Let's look at some of these verses.

dekho to kis ravaani se kahte hain she'r Mir
dur se hazaar chand hai un ke sukhan mein aab

Look, with what a flow of words
Mir recites his couplets.
There is more lustre in his verse
than in pearls.

jalvah hai mujhi se lab-e dariaaye sukhan par
sad rang meri mauj hai main tab'a-e ravaan huun

All the marvels
on the lips of the river
owe their origin to me.
My tide has a hundred colours.
I am always surging and
creatively flowing.

In the opening couplet of the following ghazal, Mir explicitly compares his verse to an overflowing river.

Mir dariya hai sune she'r zabaani us ki
allah allah re tabiiyat ki ravaani us ki!

Mir resembles a river.
We have heard him recite.
By the grace of God,

his temperament
is a gush of creativity.

baat ki tarz ko dekho to koi jaadu tha
par mili khaak mein kya sehr bayaani us ki

The style of his conversation
was really enchanting.
But his magical capabilities
dissolved into dust.

sar-guzasht apni kis andoh se shab kehta tha
so gaye n suni aah kahaani us ki

Last night,
he was telling his story
with great grief.
But you fell sleep.
Alas, you didn't hear his tale
of heart-rending woe.

marsiye dil ke kaaii kah ke diye logon ko
shahr dilli mein hai sab paas nishaani us ki

He composed heartfelt elegies
and gave them to his friends.
In the city of Dilli everyone
has them as his imprint.

aable ki si tarah thes lagi phuut bahe
dard mandi mein gaaii saari javaani us ki

He was hit like a blister
and the wound leaked.
He spent all his life
in distress and suffering.

Natural Flow of Smooth Structures

duube uchhle hai aaftaab hanuuz
kahien dekha hai us ko dariya par

The sun is leaping and vaulting today.
Maybe, it saw her bathing on the river.

The verbal structures of Mir's poetry, as elaborated above, reveal his latent talent of writing with a natural flow. His verse is very close to basic conversational patterns. Words and phrases used by him show his preference for a conversational style, but it is not mere conversation as we would see later. If he made any changes anywhere to this basic mode, the purpose was to reinforce the essence. The first few couplets in this section are mystical but are written in an intimate style.

sarsari tum jahaan se guzre
varna har ja jahaan-e diigar tha

You passed through the world
rather casually.
There was a world
within the world that you missed.

gosh ko hosh se tuk khol ke sun shor-e jahaan
sab ki aavaaz ke parde mein sukhan saaz hai ek

Open the ears of your consciousness for a while
and hear intently with deep attentiveness
to the subtle tumult of sounds of this world.
Behind the noise of these thousand voices,
there is one and only one underlying note,
that of the invisible all-pervasive melody-maker.

bekhudi le gaaii kahaan ham ko
der se intizaar hai apna

My subliminal unconsciousness
took me to an unknown place.
I have been waiting for myself
for quite some time.

ve log tu ne ek hi shokhi mein kho diye
paida kiye the charkh ne jo khaak chhaan kar

You lost those people
in a single random playful action—
Those rarest of the rare ones
who were created by the heavens,
after straining a whole lot of particles
for centuries.

maut ik maandagi ka vaqfa hai
yaa'ni aage chalein ge dam le kar

Death is a momentary pause.
We shall move forward
after a little bit of rest.

bahut sa'ii kiije to mar rahiye Mir
bas apna to itna hi maqduur hai

If you put in great effort, Mir,
you can choose to die.
Yes, that is the limit of your power.

aa'lam aaiina hai jis ka vo mussavvir be-badal
haae kya parde mein tasviirein banaata hai miyaan

The one who holds a mirror to the world
is an artist without a comparison.
What beautiful faces He paints on the canvas, Miyan!

u'mr bhar ham rahe sharaabi se
dil-e pur khuun ki ik gulaabi se

I was inebriated most of my life.
A little pink goblet filled with blood
simply stayed on my heart forever.

ji dhaha jaaye hai sahar se aah
raat guzre gi kis kharaabi se

Alas! My heart is crestfallen
since the morning.

I wonder how awful
the night would be.

khilna kam kam kali ne siikha hai
us ki aankhon ki niim-khwaabi se

The bud opens slowly, very slowly.
Who do you think she learnt it from?
From my beloved's half-open
And dreamy eyes, of course.

burqa uth-te hi chaand sa nikla
daagh huun us ki be-hijaabi ka

When she uncovered her face
I saw a moon rise.
The dazzle of her shimmering beauty
hit my heart and it left a scar.

kaam the i'shq mein bahut par Mir
ham hi faarigh huye shitaabi se

There was a lot to be done in love, Mir,
but my luck did not get an opportunity
and I lost everything.

saaqi tuk ek mausam-e gul ki taraf bhi dekh
tapka pare hai rang chaman mein hava se aaj

Saqi, please take a break and
look at the spring season.

The air is spraying colour
on the garden.

ham huye tum huye k Mir huye
us ki zulfon ke sab asiir hue

Whether it is you, or I,
or simply Mir,
we are all prisoners
of her tresses.

barhtein nahien palak se ta-ham talak bhi pahunchein
phirti hain vo nigaahein palkon ke saae saaye

Her bewitching sights
do not go beyond
her eyelids to reach me.
They stay veiled
under the shadow
of her eyelashes.

har qit'a-e chaman par tuk gaar kar nazar ko
bigrien hazaar shaklein tab phuul y banaaye

Look deeply and carefully
at each section of the garden.
How many beauties were scuffed?
Only then these captivating flowers
came into being.

samjhe the ham to Mir ko aa'shiq usi ghari
jab sun ke tera naam vo betaab sa hua

We knew Mir to be your lover
the moment he heard your name
and became restless.

hai junmbish-e lab mushkil jab aan ke vo baithe
jo chaahein so yuun kah lein log apni jagah baithe

It is difficult to move lips
when she comes and sits here.
The onlookers may say
whatever they want
while sitting awestruck,
wherever they are.

kya rang mein shokhi hai us ke tan-e naazuk ki
pairaahan agar pahne to us p bhi teh baithe

What brightness of colour
emanates from her delicate body!
If she wears an apparel
even that would carry
a gleam of pink.

jin balaaon ko Mir sunte the
un ko is rozgaar mein dekha

The stories of calamities
that you had only heard, Mir,
you also saw them
in the real world.

guundh ke goya patti gul ki vo tarkiib banaaii hai
rang badan ka tab dekho jab choli bhiige pasiine mein

After kneading petals of roses,
a concoction was prepared.
That is the colour of her skin
when her blouse is soaking
with her sweat.

ham faqiiron se be-adaaii kya
aan baithe jo tum ne pyaar kiya

Why do you overlook
mendicants like us?
We came and sat here
since you showed some love.

jam gaya khuun kaf-e qaatil p tera Mir zabas
un ne ro ro diya kal haath ko dhote dhote

Your blood froze
on the palm of the murderer, Mir.
She cried as she washed her hands,
yesterday morning.

zulm hai qehr hai qayaamat hai
ghusse mein us ke zer-e lab ki baat

It is oppression.
It is cruelty.
It is a doomsday.
When in anger,
she curses quietly
under her breath.

yaaquut koi in ko kahe hai koi gul-barg
tuk honth hila tu bhi k ik baat thahar jaaye

Some call them a ruby,
others call them a rose petal.
You need to say something
so that this matter is settled.

jab naam tera liije tab chashm bhar aave
is zindagi karne ko kahaan se jigar aave

When I utter your name,
my eyes fill with tears.
From where I can get the heart
to lead such a life?

mere saliiqe se meri nibhi mohabbat mein
tamaam u'mr main naakaamion se kaam liya

My discreet disposition
helped me in my love.
All my life, I faced one failure
after another.

duur baitha ghubaar-e Mir us se
i'shq bin y adab nahien aata

Mir sat at a distance
like a cloud of dust.
Without falling in love
you can't learn this etiquette.

sakht kaafir tha jis ne pehle Mir
mazhab-e i'shq ikhtiyaar kiya

He was solidly a kafir—
the one who embraced,
from the beginning,
the religion of love.

massaaib aur the par ji ka jaana
a'jab ik saaniha sa ho gaya hai

There were other sufferings too,
but the day I lost my heart
it was an inexplicable accident.

chashm-e khuun basta se kal raat lahu phir tapka
ham ne jaana tha k bas ab to y naasuur gaya

My eyes filled with blood
once again leaked last night.
I had assumed that my unhealed wounds
had been healed.

A Deceptive Simplicity

n rakho kaan nazm-e shaa'iraan-e haal par itne
chalo tuk Mir ko sun-ne k moti se pirota hai

Don't pay too much attention
to poets of the day.
Let us go and listen to Mir.
He does not use words.
He beads pearls in his poetry.

Mir's simplicity is truly quite deceptive. There is an impression that simplicity of the syntactic structure equals simplicity of poetic meaning which is not correct. Mir speaks in a dialogic language that seems conversational, but his simplicity is deceptive. It is an established fact that conversational language is not poetry's language. The poetic language infused with creative devices when removed from the language of daily discourse becomes more meaningful and durable. Mir selected a mode of expression that connected him with the people, but he moulded it metaphorically into a 'deep structured' and creative language. He was using conversational usage, but at the same time he chiselled it as a fine-cut diamond that made it distinctive. What is the secret? Let see how Mir has alluded to this question:

shaa'yir nahien jo dekha tu to hai koi saahir
do chaar she'r parh kar sab ko rijha gaya hai

Not seen a poet like you.
You are a magician.
You read a few couplets,
and everyone was moved.

she'r mere hain sab khwaas pasand
par mujhe guftagu a'vaam se hai

My artistry is liked
by the sophisticated.
But I address
the common folks.

The spoken language of the time, Rekhta, was an imperfect hybrid language, created by the forces of social synthesis and history; it was a language in the making. How did Mir overcome those deficiencies and turned it into an art form? He addresses this question with some pride:

dil kis tarah n khenchein ash'aar rekhte ke
behtar kiya hai main ne is a'ib ko hunar se

Poetry written in Rekhta—
there wasn't much to like there.

I have made it lustrous—
something imperfect reshaped
with my ingenuity.

And also:

kya jaanun dil ko khenche hain kyon she'r Mir ke
kuchh tarz aisi bhi nahien iihaam bhi nahien

I can't say why Mir's verse attracts one's heart.
There is nothing on the surface that explains it.
No play of words or brassy craftiness,
yet it is fabulous and creates an effect!

Conversational Creativity

If Mir speaks in a simple conversational language and there are
no special devices that he uses, then what is the secret behind
the 'pearls in his poetry'? This question draws attention to a
critical aspect of poetic language—although conversational
language by itself is not poetic language, poetic language can
be conversational. The way it is done entirely depends on the
poet's ingenuity. It is true that Mir adopted a conversational
style, but he didn't use it at the level of ordinary conversation.
The difference between the two rests on a fundamental
distinction: ordinary language operates at the surface.
Words mean other words. They communicate the message,
then fizzle out and vanish. In the poetic language, words
communicate at the surface level and at a deeper metaphoric
level; there are also other levels of association, denotation, and

connotation in which meaning is conveyed. Poetic language hides within itself a deep structure, sometimes even layers of deep structures.

Mir touched upon only the prevalent rhetorical aspects while discussing his andaaz in his *Tazkirah Nikaat-us Sho'ra* but, as we know, good poetry goes beyond any rhetorical system and, in fact, its deep structures often create new forms of associated sub-structures. It is not necessary that a poet is conscious of all the aesthetic or innovative aspects of what he has created. It often opens new doors of feelings and impressions, emotions and modes of thinking which are outside the range of the surface structure. The latter describe only physical aspects of reality. Words are limited, but meanings have no boundaries. Or one may say, the words are finite while the meanings are infinite.

Jaques Lacan, a French philosopher, who followed in Freud's footsteps, but differed from him significantly, held that structures of language are in fact structures of human unconsciousness. This indicates that darker zones of language are more compelling than the brighter zones. The limits of the darker zones can't be known. The scope of the spoken language, as we know, is limited to a few hundred pages of a dictionary. The real artistry of an artist is to create something extraordinary with the limited lexicon of commonly used words.

Words per se are neither ordinary nor extraordinary. It is their usage that makes them so, including a touch of creativity such as 'He beads pearls in his poetry'. What Mir is claiming in the couplets mentioned above is that he feels intuitively. He himself is wonderstruck at what he has achieved. He is proud of the *effect*, of what has been created in a gush. Undoubtedly, the author himself is the first private reader, that is why he may revise, chisel or refine the text, sometimes more than once. But the sum total of the readers over the years form the reception of the writer. The French literary critic Roland Barthes was of the opinion that the writer and their work can only propose meanings; it is the reader who disposes them. Criticism itself is nothing but reading. But all the readers are not at the same level. There are sophisticated and informed readers as well as non-critical readers. Firaq Gorakhpuri is reported to have said that in the case of Mir everything ordinary becomes extraordinary. Ordinary language does not remain ordinary language; it is transformed into a magical poetic language that has multiple meanings.

Function of Deep Structures

sahl hai Mir ka samajhana kya
har sukhan us ka ik muqaam se hai

It is not easy to grasp Mir's work.
Each verse is from somewhere—
unknown and unknowable.

zulf sa pechdaar hai har she'r
hai sukhan Mir ka a'jab dhab ka

Every *she'r* is like the ringlet
of the beauty's curly tresses.
Mir's verse is of a different class.

What is the true significance of the ringlets of curly tresses, or putting pearls into a string, or creating magic that astounds the reader? One process of the transformation of the ordinary into the extraordinary is relational. Relationships between words and their meanings are created with the help of some already available poetic devices and modes. But Mir creatively makes use of additional modes which have no given name. Mir's special ability lies in the fact that he brings to surface deeper structures to mesh with the ordinary speaking language. He does this with an incredible skill without making the reader conscious of this change.

kaha main ne kitna hai gul ka sabaat
kali ne y sun kar tabassum kiya

I asked the rose bud,
'How long is the life of a flower?'
The bud listened and smiled.

At the surface, the language of the couplet above is quite ordinary. But if we look closely there is a world of meaning hidden behind it. The reference to rose, bud, or the flower itself is not extraordinary as such references are commonly found in Urdu poetry. But there are few things which are quite extraordinary. First, there is the quality of the dialogue itself. The question comes from a living voice and it is directed towards a non-living entity. Second, the answer is not given in words; the only response of the bud is a smile followed by silence. Third, the smile can be interpreted in many ways. A smile is sometimes an answer to a question that has no logical answer. Perhaps, the bud smiles because it is excited about becoming a flower. Beyond this meaning, there is an array of other meanings that includes reaching the pinnacle of beauty with full flowering and the march of the flower towards its gradual decline and demise. The beauty of a flower in full bloom will not last forever. The smile is a metaphor for a momentary life, a life which will last only as long as a smile lasts. The spring too proverbially is not going to be around for long.

Thus, we see in Mir's hands ordinary language goes through a creative transformation. The answer to the question 'how long is the life of a flower?' is as obvious as the sun. The hidden structures of meanings create delight and add to the lancet-like quality of the couplet. Many early critics who did not go beyond the surface reading of Mir's work readily came to the conclusion that he is a poet of simplicity and conversational language. Yet Mir himself left the critics such clear signs.

koi saadah hi us ko saadah kahe
hamein to lage hai vo a'iyyaar sa

Only simple folks would call him simple.
To me, he is artful and masterly.

The 'artful and masterly' part got a little attention and critics continued to follow the easy path of simple classification. Let us take a look at some more couplets:

sub-h tak sham'a sar ko dhunti rahi
kya patange ne iltimaas kiya

The candle was ecstatic
and flickering
until morning.
Wonder, what entreaties
the moth made to her?

masaaib aur the par dil ka jaana
a'jab ik saaniha sa ho gaya hai

There was no dearth of calamities,
but losing my heart
was a strange accident altogether!

rang-e gul o buue gul hote hain hava donon
kya qaafila jaata hai jo tu bhi chala chaahe

Colours of roses
and the fragrance of flowers
are fading away.
What a caravan departs
as you are leaving!

use dhuundte Mir khoe gaye
koi dekhe is justuju ki taraf

Mir lost himself in his search.
Someone should think about
the mystery of his endeavour.

paas-e naamuus-e i'shq tha varna
kitne aansu palak tak aaye the

I was concerned about my dignity
and restraint as a lover.
Otherwise, a lot of tears had hit my eyelid.

y tavahhum ka kaarkhaana hai
yaan vohi hai jo e'tibaar kiya

This is a world of fantasy.
Everything is illusive.
Whatever you believe is real.

chashm ho to aaiina-khaana hai dahr
munh nazar aate hain diivaaron ke biich.

If you have eyes,
this world is like a house of mirrors.
You can see faces upon faces
in the walls.

shaam se kuchh bujha sa rehta hai
dil hua hai charaagh muflis ka

When evening comes
my heart loses its verve.
It starts to quiver
like a poor man's lamp.

ek mahruum chale Mir hamien aa'lam se
varna aa'lam ko zamaane ne diya kya kya kuchh

Mir, I was the only one
who departed deprived and excluded.
The world did a lot for others.

marg-e majnun p a'ql gum hai Mir
kya divaane ne maut paaii hai

The death of Majnun, Mir
makes me lose myself in disbelief.
Can a lover like him ever die?

ho ga kisi diivaar ke saaye ke tale Mir
kya kaam mohabbat se us aaraam talab ko

Mir must be squatting somewhere,
under the shadow of a wall.
What has that carefree to do with love?

aa'dam-e khaaki se aa'lam ko jila hai varna
aaiina tha y vale qaabil-e diidaar n tha

The world received this bright glow
from the ash of Adam.
Otherwise, this house of mirrors
was not worth watching.

hain musht-e khaak lekin jo kuchh hain Mir ham hain
maqduur se zayaada maqduur hai hamaara

We are simply a fistful of ashes
but whatever there is,

Mir is conscious of his self.
The destiny that we make
is more than what is ordained.

sar kisi se firo nahien hota
haif bande hue khuda n hue

It is really difficult
to give up self-esteem.
Alas, I am man, not a god!

maahiiyat-e do aa'lam khaati phire hai ghote
yak qatrah khuun-e dil y tuufaan hai hamaara

The reality of this world and the other
is revolving and disappearing again and again.
This storm is wrought by one tiny drop of blood
which we call heart.

Mir was conscious of his pervasive ingenuity. Following
couplets affirm this:

khush hain diivaangi-e Mir se sab
kya junuun kar gaya sha'uur se vo

All are happy
with Mir's strange madness.
His surprising psychosis
and stunning creativity!

tarfein rakhe hai ek sukhan chaar chaar Mir
kya kya kaha karein hain zabaan-e qalam se ham

Each couplet of Mir reveals
multiple dimensions of creativity.
Isn't it amazing how much a poet could say
just with the tip of an ordinary reed pen?

tha bala hangaama-aara Mir bhi
ab talak galion mein us ka shor hai

What a turbulent marvel
Mir really was!
His amazing words
still keep echoing in the streets.

amiir zaadon se dilli ke mil n taa-maqduur
k ham faqiir hue hain inhien ki daulat se

Do not expect much good
from the aristocrats of Dilli.
People like us are dirt poor
because of their wealth.

sann'a hain sab khwaar azaan jumla huun main bhi
hai a'ib bara us mein jise kuchh hunar aave

Artists are treated terribly in this world.
That has been my lot too.

The one who attains something extraordinary
is the one considered deficient.

jalva hai mujhi se lab-e dariya-e sukhan par
sad rang meri mauj hai main taba'e ravaan huun

On the banks of the river of poetry,
all delights flow from me.
My tide has every colour of the heart.
I am the river roaring and gushing.

turfa sann'a hain ae Mir y mauzon tabaa'n
baat jaati hai bigar to bhi bana dete hain

Amazing are these artists, Mir!
How spontaneous is their creativity!
If something goes wrong,
they mend it right away.

Mir sann'a hai milo is se
dekho baatein to kya banaata hai

Look what an artist Mir is!
You should meet him.
He weaves magic in his words.

Conversational Chatter of Mir Soz and Kitchen Girls

People with a deep understanding of the genesis of poetry
called Mir *muhaavara daan-e matiin* (a great master of

idiomatic language) because his poetry had a perfectionistic multidimensional touch. Those who wrote *Tazkirahs* found the use of idiom a distinguishing feature, but the reality is that the idiom is only one of the components in the totality of things. There are many inventive avenues that are open to a poet. Mir makes use of all the options to create poetic meaningfulness and to paint compelling images of ordinary as well as extraordinary aspects of existence. He shows real craftsmanship in effectively presenting the most intricate human emotions. Mohammad Husain Azad rightly wrote about this in his book *Aab-e Hayaat:* 'Mir might have borrowed the conversational style from Soz, but the latter mainly dealt with the way people talked. Mir filled this talk with content and context and gave it depth and dignity and thus made it inventive for sharing it in an assembly.'[1]

The above discussion leads to the question: How do we add content into a conversation? Doesn't customary conversation already contain content? Does it mean that this conversation lacks meaningfulness? On the surface, it seems that Azad made up a story to distinguish Mir from Soz. This has been a matter of some debate among people who have written about Mir. Even if we agree that Mir was influenced by Soz, his poetry is totally different.

Mir was aware and even conceited about his creativity. *Tazkirah-e Khush Ma'rka-e Zeba* narrates an interesting incident that happened at the Royal Court in Lucknow. One day, Nawab Asif-ud Daula asked Soz, who was the king's teacher, to recite some poetry. Soz recited two or

---

[1]   Azad, *Aab-e Hayaat*, p. 208.

three ghazals. The Nawab showered praise on his teacher. Whatever the king does, courtiers join him. So there were a lot of *wah wah*s. This irritated Mir who was present there. He took it as an affront. After a while, Mir cornered Soz and asked him how he could recite ghazal upon ghazal when a master-poet like Mir was present in the assembly. Soz respectfully answered, 'This humble person is no less a poet, Sir, and like you I too belong to Delhi.' This further infuriated Mir and he told Soz, 'The right place for your poetry is not the King's Court or the majestic presence of Mir, but a backyard kitchen where young girls giggle and chatter while they do their bubbly cooking in earthen pots.' This incident shows how deeply proud Mir was of having perfected his multifaceted style which was different from the raw conversational craft of poets like Soz. And he was not apologetic about this.

kya tha rekhta pardah sukhan ka
so thahra hai vohi ab fan hamaara

I picked up Rekhta
as a veil for my poetry.
To make a confession,
that is my artistry now.

Al-e Ahmed Suroor's assessment that when we compare Soz with Mir we realize the extent of Mir's grasp and artistry is quite correct. Soz deals with cold ash. But in Mir's poetry the ash turns into molten liquid that touches one's inner self. Mir called conversational language *guftaar-e khaam* (half-formed language), but when he forges it in the fire of agony within his heart, it turns into great poetry.

be soz-e dil kinhon ne kaha rekhta to kya
guftaar-e khaam pesh-e aziizaan sanad nahien

Many poets use Rekhta
without adding a piece of their burning heart.
The half-baked conversational language
is not a measure of poetic creativity.

There is a hidden fire in Mir's compositions. Neither the way he speaks, nor his style has the feel of ordinary. He draws his essence from the depths of the ground he walks on. That is how he separates himself from other poets of his time who suffered from lack of substance and perfection. The following couplets are a proof of these assertions:

Mir shaay'ir bhi zor koi tha
dekhte ho n baat ka usluub

Mir was a wonderful poet.
You should have noticed
his superb creative mannerism.

a'jab hote hain shaay'ir bhi main is firqe ka aa'shiq huun
k be dharke bhari majlis mein y asraar kehte hain

People consider poets strange beings.
I'm a poet who belongs to that tribe.

They speak about things that are surreptitious
in assemblies openly and courageously.

shart saliiqa hai har ik amr mein
ai'b bhi karne ko hunar chaahiye

Sleek mannerism is a precondition
for accomplishing every piece of work.
Perfection is needed even for doing
a wrong thing.

kis ka hai qimaash aisa guudar bhare hain saare
dekho n jo logon ke divan nikalte hain

Who has any competence?
Look at the people, full of crap.
Those who publish their divans
day in, day out.

The following Mir couplet about the centredness of *nazar*
(discriminating look) is based on his habitual deep insight. It
is wonderful in many respects.

qalab yaa'ni k dil a'jab zar hai
is ki naqqaadi ko nazar hai shart

The centre of my being,
also called the heart,
is as precious as gold.
To discern it,

you need an eye
that can place a jewel.

To give a few examples of excellent couplets by Mir is a
challenging task because each couplet is memorable and can
easily be added to a list of quotable quotes.

qadr rakhti n thi mataa'-e dil
saare aa'lam ko main dikha laaya.

The wealth of the heart
commanded little recognition.
I showed it to the whole world
but there was no true buyer.

ek do hon to sehr-e chashm kahuun
kaarkhaana hai vaan to jaadu ka

If it were one or two,
I would call it the allurement of eyes.
There is a whole world of wizardry here.

iltefaat-e zamaana par mat ja
Mir deta hai rozgaar fareb

Don't be misled
by the kindness of the world.
Mir, this world is full of traps.

ustukhwaan kaamp kaamp jalte hain
i'shq ne aaag y lagaaii hai

My bones burn and shiver.
What a fire love has ignited!

hairat-e husn-e yaar se chup huun
sab se harf o kalaam hai mauquuf

Due to a feeling of wonder and awe
caused by the beloved's beauty
I have been rendered speechless
in the assembly of friends.

khush n aaii tumhaari chaal hamein
yuun n karna tha paaemaal hamein

I am a victim
of your manner of walking.
You should not have crushed
me in this manner.

shahr-e khuubi ko khuub dekha Mir
jins-e dil ka kahien rivaaj nahien

I went through the city of beauty
in great detail.
There are no takers
for a commodity like a heart.

us ke iifaae a'hd tak n jiye
u'mr ne ham se bevafaaii ki

I did not live long enough
to see her fulfil her promise.
Alas, life proved so treacherous!

chhor jaate hain dil ko tere paas
y hamaara nishaan hai pyaarey

I leave my heart
in your custody.
Take it as my souvenir,
dear one!

ae shor-e qayaamat ham sote hi n rah jaavein
is raah se nikle to ham ko bhi jaga jaana

O tumult of the doomsday,
don't leave me behind while I'm sleeping.
When you pass this way,
make sure that you wake me up.

masaaib aur the par dil ka jaana
a'jab ik saaniha sa ho gaya hai

There were other calamities,
but the loss of my heart—
it was a disaster
of a different kind.

vajah-e begaangi nahien maa'luum
tum jahan ke ho vaan ke ham bhi hain

I don't know the cause
of your estrangement.
I belong to the same place
where you come from.

aage kisu ke kya karein dast-e tam'a daraaz
vo haath so gaya hai sarhaane dhare dhare

How should I extend my hand
before someone for begging?
That hand has become numb
after staying long under the head.

kare kya k dil bhi to majbuur hai
zamiin sakht hai aasmaan duur hai

What can the poor heart do?
It is helpless.
The ground below is hard,
and the sky above is far away.

bahut sa'ii kariye to mar rahiye Mir
bas apna to itna hi maqduur hai

If you want to put in a lot of effort,
the most you can do is die, Mir.
That is the outreach of human destiny.

A Delightful Synthesis of Persian and Rekhta

laaya hai mera shauq mujhe parde se baahar
main varna vohi khilvati-e raaz-e nihaan huun

My passion brought me out from the veil.
Otherwise, I am the same secret—
a tiny secret among all the secrets.

The emphasis on Mir's simplicity came at the cost of other significant aspects of his poetry. When Maulvi Abdul Haq and Asar Lakhnavi wrote about it, this line of thinking gained popularity. But it is rather strange that this critique continued even until Syed Abdullah, who wrote about Mir much later. He wrote, 'There is no doubt that when Mir shows the Persian influence, he reveals something new and innovative, but this is not his original colour. There, something is missing.' What this meant was that the appeal of Mir's poetry essentially depends on the simplicity of his style. This view is highly limiting and may be viewed as an attempt to pigeon-hole the span of Mir's work. He is simple and complex; he plays at the surface, but then he also reaches great depths. The following ghazal, written in an accomplished Persian style, is an excellent example of his strength:

main kaun huun ae ham-nafasaan sokhta jaan huun
ik aag mere dil mein hai jo sho'la fishaan huun

Who am I, my sweet friends?
One with a burnt-out heart.
There is a fire that burns inside.
I am a walking inferno.

However Abdullah commented, 'this couplet is complete and without any fault. It could have been written by any of the medieval masters such as Kalim or Salim. But this verse lacks the special quality and flavour that we usually find in Mir.'[1] It is surprising how as a serious reader of Mir's poetry, Syed Abdullah, ignored some exceedingly beautiful, creative and well-crafted couplets from the same ghazal. This effort to look for only one kind of 'quality and flavour' in Mir was misplaced.

laaya hai mera shauq mujhe parde se baahar
main varna vohi khilvati-e raaz-e nihaan huun

My passion brought me out from the veil.
Otherwise, I am the same secret—
a tiny secret among all the secrets.

---

[1] Abdullah, *Naqde Mir,* p. 22.

jalvah hai mujhi se lab-e dariya-e sukhan par
sad rang meri mauj hai main tab'e ravaan huun

I am the spectacle
on the shore of the ocean of poetry.
My tides show multiple colours
and I flow immaculately.

ik vahm nahien besh meri hasti-e mauhuum
is par bhi teri khaatir-e naazuk p garaan huun

My existence is nothing more
than a deception, a flicker of a thought.
Still I am a burden, an affliction
for your delicate heart.

Most often, Mir fulfils the strict and extremely ingenious requirement of Persian versification. There are many highly creative Persian-based phrases that we usually associate with Ghalib like *kaav kaav, yak qatr-e khuun, saada o purkaar, shiisha baaz, yak biyabaan, hangaama garm-kun, hariif-e be-jigar, hariif-e nabard,* etc. as pointed out by Asar Lakhnavi. But we forget the fact that they were originally crafted by Mir; and Ghalib and others borrowed them from him, as can be seen from the following couplets:

yak biyabaan ba-rang-e saut-e jaras
mujh p hai bekasi o tanhaaii

The faint caravan bells in the desert
melt into the darkness—

broken and helpless like me,
sad and forlorn!

hangaama garm-kun jo dil-e na-subuur tha
paida har ek naale se shor-e nushuur tha

The tumult caused
by the impatient heart
produced lamentation
that was no less than the noise
of the day of judgement.

aavaargaan-e i'shq ka puuchha jo main nishaan
musht-e ghubaar le ke saba ne ura diya

When I inquired
the fate of unfortunate
forlorn lovers,
the wind took hold
of a handful of dust
and flew it into the air.

dil k yak qatra-e khuun nahien hai besh
ek aa'lam ke sar bala laaya

The heart might not be
in excess of a drop of blood,
but it has brought calamity and ruin
to the whole world.

dil i'shq ka hamesha hariif-e nabard tha
ab jis jagah k daagh hai vaan aage dard tha

The heart always gave up
in the battle of love.
Where there is a scar now
was once the seat of pain.

Delightful Flavouring of Persian

The structure of couplets quoted above travelled straight from Mir to Ghalib. Both of these great poets of Urdu belonged to Agra. In Mir's Divans, there is no shortage of couplets that contain a delightful mix of Persian phrases and colloquial Rekhta. The charm of his couplets rested on the hybrid amalgamation of Persian words with the syncretic and colloquial structures of Rekhta. Whenever and wherever Mir confronted cataclysms and misfortunes, he went deeper into his self, or he dived into metaphysics and talked about the mystery of existence, or he drowned himself into the wonders of contemplation. He often delved into a combination of Persian and Prakrit figures of speech. There is no difference of opinion that these couplets are among his best and in comparison to his other couplets, there is no dearth of a 'lancet-like pointedness' in such couplets as well.

zabaan rakh ghuncha saan apne dahan mein
bandhi muthi chala ja is chaman mein

Keep your tongue in your mouth,
like a bud keeps itself closed.
Do walk through the garden freely
as you may like, but keep your secrets
firmly inside you like a fist closed.

mausam aaya to nakhl-e daar mein Mir
sar-e mansuur hi ka baar aaya

When the season came for the sacrifice, Mir,
the fruit that the desert palms bore
was actually the hanging head of Mansur![2]

kuchh gul se hain shagufta kuchh sarv se hain qad kash
us ke khayal mein ham dekhe hain khwaab kya kya

Some are more cheerful than flowers,
some are like cypress trees.
Thinking of her beauty
what amazing dreams have I seen!

chashm ho to aaiina-khaana hai dahr
munh nazar aata hai diivaaron ke biich

If you have eyes,
this world is like a house of mirrors.
You can see faces upon faces
in the walls.

---

[2] Mansur Al-Hallaj, a Persian Sufi mystic, was beheaded for claiming *Ana'l-Haqq* (I'm the Truth) in 922 AD.

y a'ish-gah nahien hai yaan rang aur kuchh hai
har gul hai is chaman ka saaghar bhara lahu ka

This world is not a place
for merriment.
Beware of the colours!
Each flower is a goblet
filled with blood.

sarv-e lab-e ju laala o gul nasriin o saman hain shaguufe bhi
dekho jidhar ik baagh laga hai apne rangiin khayaalon ka

The tall cypresses
near flowing waters,
tulips and flowers,
white roses and jasmines.
Wherever I look,
there is a garden
of my colourful imagination.

va us se sar-e harf to ho go k y sar jaaye
ham halq-e buriidah hi se taqriir karein ge

Let there be dissent
even if the head is to be offered.
The word must be uttered
even if it has to come from
a severed head.[3]

---

[3] A veiled reference to Karbla tragedy.

kare hai jis ko mulaamat jahaan vo main hi huun
ajal rasiida jafa diidah iztiraab zadah

Profusely admonished
is none other than me.
The one who is condemned to death,
the one who has been deceived,
the one who is in terrible agony,
is none other than me.

maahiiyat-e do aa'lam khaati phire hai ghote
yak qatrah khuun-e dil y tuufaan hai hamaara

The existence of this world
and the other is sinking
and resurfacing in the tumult
of the ocean of thought.
A tiny drop of blood in the heart
and all this terrible tempest!

zulm hai qehr hai qayaamat hai
ghusse mein us ke zer-e lab ki baat

It is oppression.
It is cruelty.
It is a doomsday.
When in anger,
she curses quietly
under her breath.

is dasht mein ae sail sambhal hi ke qadam rakh
har samt ko yaan dafn meri tashna-labi hai

In this barren land, O flood,
be careful if you dare tread.
Be careful wherever you go,
you will find my thirst
buried underneath.[4]

maa'luum tere chehra-e purnuur ka sa lutf
bilfarz aasmaan p gaya phuul maah hua

I know the pleasure
of your luminous face.
A flower went up the sky
and it blossomed as moon.

maa-nind-e harf safah-e hasti se uth gaya
dil bhi mera jariidah-e aa'lam mein fard tha

Like a word, it got erased
from the book of existence.
My heart was one of its kind
in the journal of the world.

chaahe jis shakl se timsaal sifat is mein dar aa
aa'lam aaiine ke maanind dar-e baaz hai ek

---

4   Another reference to Karbla.

You can enter in any form or shape,
this world is like a house of mirrors—
with only one door and no exit.

More than any other contemporary poet, Mir was influenced
by the phraseology of the Persian ghazal and he grafted it well
into the Urdu verse. Urdu, we should remember, was still a
developing language. Many of the Persian phrases and idioms
in Mir's poetry slowly became a part of this evolving language.
Such phrases may run into hundreds. Here are a few examples:

Persian	Urdu
khush aamdan	*khush aana* (to like)
bar-ruue kaar aavardan	*baruue kaar laana* (to use)
tamaasha kardan	*tamasha karna* (to see)
saaz kardan	*saaz karna* (to suit)
niyaaz kardan	*niyaaz karna* (to offer)

Waheeduddin Saleem has compiled a full list of such phrases
that are found in Mir's work. These phrases were later used by
Ghalib and he earned notoriety for them. Let us look at some
free-flowing lyrical word combinations:

sehra sehra vahshat (madness everywhere)
duniya duniya tohmat (world being thought, only a thought)
aa'lam aa'lam i'shq o junuun (whole world being love and madness)
josh-e ashk-e nadaamat (to be full of tears of remorse)
ghuubaare diidah-e parvana (haze in the eyes of the moth)
sar nashiin raah-e mai-khaana (leader in the path of tavern)

hangaama garm-kun (to celebrate the event)
harf-e zer labi (to utter something softly under the lip)

These Persian word combinations and phrases blend so well in Mir's poetry that the reader takes them as original Urdu innovations. Al-e Ahmed Suroor rightly said that Mir's style never loses its sweetness and delightful demeanour. Even mountains of izafats appear like balls of cotton. In fairness, Mir uses izafats rather sparingly in contrast to Ghalib, but his stylistic word innovations are found in abundance. Waheeduddin Saleem has a point when he says that Mir sometimes goes into very complex word formations which appear excessive in Urdu. But who could find fault with Mir's malleable lyricism? Waheeduddin Saleem has rightly noted that Mir is sometimes flexing point number four of his own *Nikaat-us Sho'ra* that says Persian phrases should be such that they have some affinity with Rekhta and that there was no better judge of this than a poet with a fine taste. Mir brings forth Persian word combinations and phrases, both familiar and unfamiliar, traditional as well as innovative, good as well as bad, but once these things go through his creative oven, they become a part of poetic Urdu. The highly creative absorption and naturalization of Persian elements in standard Urdu is a glittering spot of Mir's poetry. Let us look at couplets where we see creative transformation of Persian into literary Urdu with hardly any effort. Mir delights the reader in this task while maintaining the integrity of Urdu's *Urdupan,* i.e. Urdu's lingual genius.

sehra-e mohabbat hai qadam dekh ke rakh Mir
y sair sar-e kuucha o bazaar n hove

This is the desert of love.
You should walk carefully Mir.
This is not like strolling
in the streets and bazaars
with gay abandon.

roz aane p nahien nisbat-e i'shqi mauquuf
u'mr bhar ek mulaaqaat chali jaati hai

A loving relationship does not depend
on daily interactions.
It is a meeting of living hearts
that lasts a lifetime.

sainkron harf hain girha dil mein
par kahaan paaiye lab-e izhaar

There are hundreds of words
bundled up in the heart,
but where can the lips find
a way to express them.

jam gaya khuun kaf-e qaatil p tera Mir zabas
un ne ro ro diya kal haath ko dhote dhote

Mir, your blood froze
on the hands of the killer.
She cried bitterly
while washing her hands
again and again.

ik nigeh ek chashmak ik sukhan
is mein bhi tum ko hai ta-ammul sa

A slanted look,
a wink, a word.
Alas! even in this,
you have hesitation!

hai jo andher shahr mein khurshiid
din ko le kar charaagh nikle hai
har sahar haadisa meri khaatir
bhar ke khuun ka aayaagh nikle hai

The sun in a deserted
and ruined city rises
as if someone walks
holding a lamp
in darkness.
Each morn a new calamity,
holding a goblet
brimming with blood,
shows up looking for me.

saaye mein har palak ke khwaabiida hai qayaamat
is fitna-e zaman ko koi jaga to dekho

The calamity is sleeping and dreaming
under the shadow of her eyelids.
Who will dare to wake up
this hideously appalling beauty?

mansur ki nazar thi jo daar ki taraf so
phal vo darakht laaya aakhir sar-e buridaah

Mansur's gaze was fixed on the hanging post.
Eventually that tree bore its fruit
when the acclaimed head of Mansur
appeared there.

tuk Mir-e jigar sokhta ki jald khabar le
kya yaar bharosa hai charaagh-e sehri ka

Do inquire about the condition
of Mir's burning heart.
My friend, you can't rely much
on the morning's lamp.

kuchh mauj-e hava pechaan ae Mir nazar aaii
shaayad k bahaar aaii zanjiir nazar aaii

The wave of wind, Mir,
seemed to be curled.
Possibly spring has arrived.
I saw the chains of
those who are madly in love.

aage bhi tere i'shq se khenche the dard o ranj
lekin hamaari jaan par aisi bala n thi

My love for you had brought
untold pain and torment

in the past as well.
But my life was not as miserable
and agonized as it is now.

apne to honth bhi n hile us ke rubru
ranjish ki vajah Mir vo kya baat ho gaaii

Even the lips didn't move
when I was with her.
Mir, I don't know
what caused her indifference
and unfriendliness.

sad harf zer-e khaak tah-e dil chale gaye
mohlat n di ajal ne hamein ek baat ki

Hundreds of words in my heart
went with me as I was buried.
Death didn't give me permission
to say even one thing.

marg-e majnun se a'qal gum hai Mir
kya diivaane ne maut paaii hai

The death of Majnun, Mir
makes me lose myself in disbelief.
Can a lover like him ever die?

Urdu's First Complete Poet

aatish si phuk rahi hai saare badan mein mere
dil mein a'jab tarah ki chingaari aa pari hai

> My whole body is on fire.
> A spark of a strange kind
> has hit my heart.

For a complete understanding of Mir's poetic creativity, we have to go beyond the traditional lenses of simplicity and complexity. These classifications are too general and compartmentalized. Mir's creative mind is indifferent to such ready-made explanations. Mir was Urdu's first all-inclusive complete poet, and his work is truly multidimensional, including those aspects that unfolded in Urdu poetry long after he was gone. His metaphorical dictum was:

she'r mere hain sab khwaas pasand
par mujhe guftagu a'vaam se hai

My poetry is appreciated
by the sophisticated.

But I address
the common people.

As mentioned by Mohammad Husain Azad in *Aab-e Hayaat*,
there is a lot in Mir's works that is meant for the literati,
people with refined literary taste, and at the same time, there
is enough for common folks enjoying themselves sitting
leisurely on the steps of a crowded place like the Jam'a Masjid
in Delhi. Mir himself used 'Jam'a Masjid steps' as a metaphor
because in the changed shallow cultural environment of
Lucknow there was no concept of ordinary folks enjoying the
intricacies of refined and cultivated poetry.

Mir spent his childhood in Akbarabad, as Agra was then
known, and therefore the language that he picked up at an early
age was not the Persianized Urdu of Delhi. Still, colloquial
Urdu mixed with Braj Bhasha was the common speech in
the Agra-Mathura region. Many Braj words, expressions,
and unrefined styles that show up repeatedly in Mir's verse
and these elements remind us of an early influence that left a
permanent mark on his unconscious mind. Consider the high
frequency /o/ *or* /u/ endings or common colloquial words such
as *kabhu, kisu, kiijo, liijo, tuk, nipat, pavan, bachan, mukh,
jad, tad, in, kin, baas, nagar, birha, saanjh, sajan, maati*, etc.
He also grasped the art of selecting long vowels and stretching
the short vowels to make them musically long, a common
practice in Braj. Perhaps the knowledge of one language alone
would not have made Mir what he became. When Mir arrived
in Delhi, he carried this gift from Agra which when grafted on
to Delhi's the more refined idiom, called Khari Boli, became
the language of his early poetic expression. The influence of

Khari Boli is visible in the use of words like *aave hai, jaave hai, khaave hai, dosh uuper, ham paas, dekhiya huun,* or *jo jo tum ne sitam kiye so so ham ne uthaaye hain,* etc. Further, all these colloquial treasures were creatively kneaded into the Persian tradition prevalent during Mughal era's the twilight years. This is what bestowed a magical glow to Mir's lyricism.

The situation in Lucknow was quite different. There was a robust Awadhi influence there, as witnessed in Anis' *marsias* (elegies) and Mirza Shauq's masnavis. By the time he arrived in Lucknow, Mir was in his late sixties. It was therefore difficult for him to make a compromise based on local practices. Nonetheless, he unconsciously absorbed some Awadhi influences, and that is how he became the first complete poet of Urdu. It does not mean that Mir's command of vocabulary exceeded everyone else. Not that it matters much, no count has been made of the number of words every prominent Urdu poet knew or used. Words, a single distinct meaningful element of writing, is just one measure. Language has many layers and levels. It includes aspects which are metaphorical, syntactical, and philological. When we consider all these aspects, Mir is the only one who qualifies to be called Urdu's first complete poet. Critics, especially Rashid Ahmed Siddiqi, have mentioned that Mir's Urdu is different from other poets because while other poets rely on the use of Arabic and Persian constructs and phrases, Mir uses Urdu, pure and simple spoken Urdu with naturalized dialectal influences of the heartland of India, Agra, Delhi, and Lucknow. There is more *Urdu-iyat* (feel and ambiance of Urdu) and *Urdu-pan* (refined taste and touch of Urdu) in Mir than in any other poet. The following couplets have been specially selected to give the reader a flavour of Mir's characteristic modes of expression. The underlined words below show that it is impossible to ignore the taste and tang of homely Khari and Braj:

kahte n the mat <u>kurha</u> kar[1]
dil ho n gaya gudaaz tera

Did I not say,
'Don't scorch yourself in inner pain.'
Now, you have a molten heart.

ji <u>da-ha</u> jaaye hai sahar se aah
raat guzre gi kis kharaabi se

Alas! My heart is crestfallen
since morning.
I wonder how awful
the night would be.

lazzat se nahien khaali jaanon ka <u>khapa</u> jaana
kab khizr o masiiha ne marne ka maza jaana

Destroying yourself in the agony of love
is not without its delights.
Khizr is destined to live forever,
Jesus was hanged on the cross,
but did they ever enjoy the gratification
and the pleasure of dying.

---

[1]   *Kurha* is a typical Prakrit colloquial expression which is difficult to translate in English. It is living one's life in intense inner pain.

ek <u>dheri</u> raakh ki thi sub-h jaaye Mir par
barson se jalta tha shaayad raat jal kar rah gaya

In the morning,
it was just a pile of ash at Mir's place.
He was smouldering for years.
Probably, he went up in smoke last night.

yaaquut koi un ko kahe hai koi gul burg
tuk <u>honth</u> hila tu bhi k ik baat thahar jaaye

Some call them a ruby,
others call them a rose petal.
You need to say something
so that this matter is settled.

kya fikr karuun main k <u>tale</u> aage se gardon
y gaari meri raah mein <u>be-daul ari</u> hai

I have no peace of mind
unless the sky standing in front of me disappears.
This cart of mine, which is out of balance,
is blocking the way.

rukhsaar us ke haae re jab dekhte hain ham
aata hai ji mein aankhon ko in mein <u>giroiye</u>

O God!
When I look at her cheeks,
I have an urge to sink my eyes into them.

kya jaanuun log kahte hain kis ko suruur-e qalb
aaya nahien y lafz to hindi zabaan ke biich

I do not know what people call
the happiness of the heart.
I have not come across this word
in the Hindi language.

kah saanjh ke moye ko ae Mir rooyein kab tak
jaise charaagh-e muflis ik dam mein jal bujha tu

Mir, how long can people cry
for the one who died in the evening?
He was like a poor man's lamp;
he died suddenly.

nahien visvaas ji ganvaane ke
haae re zauq dil lagaane ke

I don't care if it is safe to give away the heart.
But alas! There is a passion hidden
in the heart yearning to die for someone.

phuul nargis ka liye bhiichak khara tha raah mein
kis ki chashm-e pur fasuun ne Mir ko jaadu kiya

Carrying a narcissus flower,
he was standing in the way
waiting for someone
whose enchanting eyes
cast a spell on Mir.

jaan ka sarfa nahien hai kuchh tujhe <u>kurhne</u> mein Mir
gham koi khaata hai meri jaan gham khaane ki tarah

When you suffer from inner pain, Mir,
you do not value your life.
Love is suffering indeed,
but must you suffer as suffering does!

tum ne dekha ho ga <u>pakpan</u> Mir ka
ham ko to aaya nazar vo khaam sahl

You may have seen Mir's ingenious perfection,
but to me it appeared simply raw and not well done.

ab chheriiye jahaan vahein goya hai dard sab
<u>phora</u> sa ho gaya hai tere gham mein tan tamaam

Wherever you touch, it pains everywhere
My entire body has turned into a blister
because of the agony of separation.

mohabbat ne khoya <u>khapaaya</u> hamein
bahut un ne dhuunda n paaya hamein

Love lost me completely.
Love consumed me totally.
They tried to search,
but they never found me.

sada ham to khoye gaye se rahe
<u>kabhu</u> aap mein tum ne paaya hamein

I was in a state of forgetfulness
most of the time.
Did you ever find me in myself?

aah-e sahar ne sozish-e dil ko mita diya
is baav ne hamein to diya sa bujha diya

Alas! The sighs at dawn
comforted the burning of my heart.
The breeze took me for a lamp
and it doused me.

dekha kahaan vo nuskha ik rog mein basa-ha
ji phir kabhu n panpa behteri kiin davaaein

Who did I see and where did I get this malady?
Thereafter, the heart didn't live long enough,
though I tried all sorts of treatments.

in dars gahon mein vo aaya n nazar ham ko
kya naql karuun khuubi us chehra kitaabi ki

I didn't see her in places
where they teach.
How can I mirror
her beautiful face
that looks just like a book.

kal baare ham se us se mulaaqaat ho gayi
do do bachan ke hone mein ik baat ho gayi

Yesterday, I had a chance meeting with her.
We exchanged a few words.
What a spellbinding experience it was!

tuk haal-e shikasta ke sunne hi mein sab kuchh hai
par vo to sukhan ras hai is baat ko kya maane

Listening to my tragic story is everything.
But she values refined words.
How can she listen to a heart-breaking tale?

andoh-e vasl o hijr ne aa'lam khapa diya
in do hi manzilon mein bahut yaar thak gaye

The whole world is weary of two things:
the pain of separation and the pleasure of the union.
These two states have enervated many friends,
though love has much more to it.

tarphe hai jab k seene mein uchhle hai do do haath
gar dil yahi hai Mir to aaraam ho chuka

It is suffering and it is jumping
wildly in my chest.
If this is the condition of your heart Mir,
then say goodbye
to any thought of comfort and relaxation.

raushan hai is tarah dil-e viiraan mein ek daagh
ujre nagar mein jaise jale hai charaagh ek

The wounds of my ruined heart
are dimly lit to give the appearance
of a lamp burning in an abandoned town.

Eternally Fresh Language

Mir's language shows its vintage, but it retains its timeless beauty. Both Urdu and Hindi have progressed a great deal during the last two hundred years, and they have embraced many new features. The days of Nasikh, who had issued strict rules for his disciples not to use certain words of local dialects (*matruuqaat*), are long over. The inclusion of slang and colloquialisms was somewhat prevalent in Delhi, and poets discovered new ways to express themselves, adding mellowness and sweetness into their expressions. Language mirrors social norms and cultural prerequisites. When social needs change and historic upheavals occur, language changes are inevitable. Every language has its baggage of archaic words and phrases that appear to be old and unsuitable for use in the changing environment. But what is the secret of Mir's language, that it does not seem old and out of date? His language is amazingly flexible. It shuns all sort of rigidity and rules do not bound it. It is soft, free, and supple. It meets the ever-changing needs of lyrical creativity. This is just the opposite of what Nasikh did to Urdu, to stem the flow and mellowness, for which a derogatory adage *Hindi ki Chindi Karna* (cleansing the language to such an extent that it loses its liveliness and freshness) is a stark reminder.

Mir's freshness is not ordinary by any means. It can be compared to the vim and vigour of blood seeping and flowing from a cut, or the melting of gold in a jeweller's forge or dewdrops settled on the petals of a newly opened flower that shiver mildly in the breeze. If Mir's lyrical language had lacked this freshness, it would not have gained prominence in several informal and creative writing ways that were revived after independence by poets like Nasir Kazmi and his contemporaries. It is not just a question of popularity. Mir's language despite its archaic elements, is not archaic itself. It is very close to the free flow and freshness of the spoken language of today. It has a deep connection with the flexible basic structure, ground realities, and the colloquial and conversational idiom of Urdu or Braj and Khari Hindi that never goes out of date. Mir's words are thus fresh today, and they will remain eternally fresh.

Rhythm and Lyricism

jo jo zulm kiye hain tum ne so so ham ne uthaaye hain
daagh jigar p jalaaye hain chhati p jaraahat khaaye hain

All your afflictions of pain
I have borne gladly—
the scars burnt on my heart
and incisions on my chest.

Mir's lyricism and its rhythmic quality are deeply rooted in the soil of the land. It is said that he creates musical effects through his careful selection of *qaafiya*s (rhyme) and *bahur* (lyrical meters, plural of bahr). He also selects *radiif*s (the last repeated word or words of each ghazal) that are long and varied, including his use of Hindi verbal radiifs that are different from those used in Arabic and Persian. According to Syed Abdullah, 'Mir used all available bahurs while composing his ghazals, but the reader draws maximum pleasure from those ghazals that have a long bahur. Such ghazals mirror subtle feelings and emotions. Mir also has a prominent role in the endeavour of preserving older Hindi lyrics (*giits*). Mir's ghazals have a delightful flavour of Prakrit Hindi giit, including the expression of personal pain and unfulfilled desires. The selection of a suitable bahur does the trick.'[2]

Let us look at some couplets:

tab the sipaahi ab hain jogi aah javaani yuun kaati
aisi thori raat mein ham ne kya kya svaang rachaaye hain

I was a soldier before I became a yogi.
Alas! How I spent my youth.
The night was short,
but I had to play many roles
in this short-lived cycles
of day and night.

mera shor sun ke jo logon ne kaha puuchhna to kahe hai kya
jise Mir kahte hain saahibo! yah vohi to khaana kharaab hai

When people heard my lyrical voice,
they inquired about my art.
O revered sirs, the person you call Mir—
he is this ruined and derelict fellow.

---

2   Syed Abdullah, *Naqd-e Mir,* p. 50.

kabhu lutf se n sukhan kiya kabhu baat kah n laga liya
yahi lahza lahza khitaab hai vohi lamha lamha itaab hai

No time to say something in a relaxed manner,
or to engage in a sweet talk.
Every moment the same way of addressing,
every moment the same annoyance to endure.

In Mir's lyricism and rhythmical versification long vowels play
an important role. He sometimes pluralizes the nominal and
verbal to create new word formations. This is made possible
by his repeated use of *nuun-ghunnah* for nasal sounds. Let us
look at the following couplets:

jafaaein dekh liyaan be vafaaiyaan dekhiin
bhala hua k teri sab buraaiyaan dekhiin

I have seen your loyalties
and I have seen your breaches of trust.
Thank goodness,
I have seen all your limitations.

dil ne hazaar rang sukhan sar kiya vale
dil se gayiin n baatein teri pyaari pyaariyaan

My words attained all the colours that were available,
but my heart could not forget your alluring conversation
filled with so much sugary sweetness.

kab se nazar lagi thi darvaaza-e haram se
pardah utha to lariyaan aankhein hamaari ham se

My gaze had been fixed
on the sanctuary's door
for a very long time.
When the veil was lifted,
my eyes found no one
other than me.

Folk Speech

With the passage of time, we have lost sight of all the
otherworldly modes that Mir used, but there are few things
that stand out as his unique innovations, and this includes the
use of ordinary spoken language, which has been transformed
into highly expressive and poetic language. Several of these
usages will not meet today's accepted grammatical norms, but
this does not diminish the importance of his creativity that is
linked to natural speech, such as *voh chale hai, voh chalein
hain, mast ho pariyaan, suuratein dikhaaiyaan, aave hai,
jaave hai, bove ga, sove ga;* or *in place of tuut gaya, tuuta gaya,
phuuta gaya; jigar aave, hunar aave;* or *dhaae kar, khaae kar*
in place of *kha kar,* etc. All these show associations with folk
speech and elongation of long vowels that render the speech
mellow, soft and sweet. As opposed to Ghalib, Mir uses fewer
izafats (ellipsis of *ka, ke, ki*), but Mir has his colloquial way of
ellipsis of post-positions, such as *mujh paas, ham paas, bulbul
kane, dil saath, der roya kiye, dil tere kuuche se aane kahe,*
instead of *aane ko, jane ko.* Mir has his own mode of dropping
of *ne,* such as, *puchha jo main nishaan, ham qiyaas kiya, baas
kiya* which are dialectical and have their mellowness and
flexibility. The underlined words in the couplets below show
the influence of folk speech:

haram ko jaaiye ya dair mein basar kariye
teri talaash mein ik dil kidhar kidhar kariye

We can spend our life in a mosque or a temple.
There is only one heart.
How can I divide it into fragments
while I'm engaged in your search?

tuk tumhaare honth ke hilne se yaan hota hai kaam
itni utni baat jo hove to maana kiijiye

Things are done right away
when you slightly move your lips.
Even if it is itsy-bitsy thing,
please show your agreement.

i'shq ki sozish ne dil mein kuchh n chhora kya kahein
lag uthi y aag naagaahi k ghar sab phuk gaya

When my heart went up in smoke,
nothing survived.
This fire started all of a sudden
and the whole house was burnt down.

ek dil ko hazaar daagh laga
androne mein jaise baagh laga

One heart suffered
thousands of blemishes.
It was like a garden
flowered within me.

rahti hai <u>chit charhi</u> hi din raat teri suurat
safhe p dil ke main ne tasviir kya nikaali

Your face is at the front and centre
of my consciousness, day and night.
On my heart's page what a picture
I have drawn!

gul ko mahbuub ham (ne) qiyaas kiya[3]
farq niqla bahut jo baas kiya

I took the rose as my beloved
But when I smelled
there was a difference.

aavaargaane i'shq ka puchha jo main (ne) nishaan
mush-te ghubaar le ke saba ne ura diya

When I inquired
the fate of unfortunate forlorn lovers,
the wind took hold of a handful of dust
and flew it into the air.

kuchh gul se hain shagufta kuchh sarv se hain qad kash
us ke khayal mein ham (ne) dekhe hain khwaab kya kya

Some are more cheerful than flowers,
some are like cypress trees.

---

[3]   Mir's use of an ellipsis indicated within parenthesis. It is an omission of
      words that is understood from contextual clues.

In thinking of her beauty
what wonderful dreams I have seen.

mat ranja kar kisi ko k apne to e'tiqaad
dil dhaaye kar jo ka'ba banaaya to kya huua

Do not hurt anyone;
this is my belief.
If you build Kaba
by breaking someone's heart,
what good is that?

jalvah-e maah tahe abr tanak bhuul gaya
un ne sote mein dupatta se jo munh ko dhaanka

The moon lost its charm
and went under the cloud
when, while still sleeping,
she covered her face with
her *dupatta*.

in gul rukhon ki qaamat lahke hai yuun hava mein
jas rang se lachakti phuulon ki daaliyaan hain

With cheeks as fresh as roses,
her flexible body swings
as colorful bough
heavy with the bloom
moves back and forth
in the morning breeze.

Mir's language is filled with several sound effects and covert musical notes, and this topic requires a more in-depth discussion. Syed Abdullah is the only scholar of Mir's poetry who has pointed out that Mir is furtively drawn to *kaaf* and *gaaf* sounds. The underlined words below showcase many ghazals that are filled with such sound effects:

aah <u>kis</u> dhab se roiiye <u>kam kam</u>
shauq had se ziyaad hai ham <u>ko</u>

Alas! How can I cry less and less.
My desire knows no limits.

khilna <u>kam kam kali</u> ne siikha hai
us ki aankhon <u>ki</u> niim-khwaabi se

The bud opens slowly, very slowly.
Who do you think she learnt it from?
From my beloved's half-open
and dreamy eyes, of course.

tujh <u>ko</u> <u>kya</u> ban-ne bigarne se zamaane <u>ke k</u> yaan
khaak <u>kin kin</u> <u>ki</u> hui aur hua <u>kya kya kuchh</u>

You are not concerned
with the upheavals that occurred.
Who was reduced to ashes
and what other things happened.

kya <u>aag</u> ki <u>chingaariyaan</u> seene mein bhari hain
jo aansu meri aankh se <u>girta</u> hai sharar hai

What sparks are hidden in my chest!
The tear that drops from my eyes
is nothing but a scintilla.

naazuki uske lab ki kya kahiye
pankhari ik gulaab ki si hai

What can I say
about the daintiness of her lips!
It's a petal of rose.
That's what it is.

Mir in niim baaz aankhon mein
saari masti sharaab ki si hai

In these half-open eyes, Mir,
there is intoxication
that surpasses the best wine.

The use of kaaf and gaaf are alluring, but features such as these
are not programmed, they are spontaneous. Mir defies any
attempt as readymade classification. His compositions are full
of creative blending and fusion.

dil ki taraf kuchh aah se dil ka lagaao hai
tuk aap bhi to aaiiye yaan zor bao hai
/ghaao hai / chhupaao hai/

Alas!
My heart is finding a loving connection
with another heart. For a moment,

you should come here because
the breeze is blowing the fire forcefully.

dil vo nagar nahien k phir aabaad ho sake
pachhtaao ge suno ho y basti ujaar ke
/ gaar ke/ ukhaar ke/

My heart is not like a town
that would see any activity again.
Listen to me,
you will regret ruining this habitat.

baaham suluuk tha to uthaate the narm garm
kaahe ko Mir koi dabe jab bigar gayi
/ ukhar gayi/ ujar gayi/

As long as we were friends,
I tolerated all misconduct.
But why should one keep enduring
when the relationship is over.

jab tak kari uthaaii gayi ham kare rahe
ek ek sakht baat p barson are rahe
/pare rahe/ khare rahe /

As long as I could bear it,
I gladly accepted it.
But for anything
that was inappropriate
I never gave any ground.

We have already mentioned Mir's use of retroflex effects that are distinctive of Indo-Dravidian languages. He captivates and enchants us with his use of simple beautifications. No feature per se is good or bad on its own. Every part can be used to create typical combinations. Some of the early post-Wali Delhi Urdu poets slowly dropped the use of everyday local sounds altogether. They acted like superior castes demanding a purity test. But fortunately, late-nineteenth and twentieth-century poets showed the courage to revolt against these unilateral decrees just like the Buddha rebelled against imposed classical lingual practices and instead used common core Prakritik Pali as the language of his discourse in place of Sanskrit. Standards are important, but if the standards become constraints, then roots of a language can dry up, and its growth can be stunted. No other poet goes back to the original roots of Urdu the way Mir does. Mir's lyrical voice is the accurate representation of those roots.

Master Rekhta Poet

rekhta rutbe ko pahunchaaya hua us ka hai
mo'taqid kaun nahien Mir ki ustaadi ka

If Rekhta reached the pinnacle of its greatness,
this was the work that he accomplished.
Is there anyone who does not accept
Mir's master mysterious touch?

Mir's real greatness lies in the fact that he was the first major poet to demonstrate the true hidden literary beauty of Urdu.

From the raw vernacular and colloquial green roots in Agra to the fusion and sophistication of Persian in Delhi and the mellow sweetness of Awadhi in Lucknow, Mir covered the whole spectrum. Firaq was right when he mentioned that Mir was the voice of all of humanity and the richness of lyrical Urdu. The magic of Mir was felt in all time-periods of Urdu's growth and development, and he got the recognition that he deserved by the title Khudaa-e Sukhan generally used by one and all. The beauty of his tone and his sensitivity to love, and the courage to face human suffering will never diminish. He gave voice to silent moments that are generally ignored, and he drew memorable pictures with words that linger in the reader's consciousness long after they stop reading or reciting a couplet or a ghazal. Mir took malleable and nearly half-baked Rekhta of the mid-eighteenth century to new heights, and with this, he reached the pinnacle of literary Urdu's poetic and creative journey.

jalva hai mujhi se lab-e daryaa-e sukhan par
sad-rang meri mauj hai main tab'e ravaan huun

I am the spectacle on the elegant river of poetry.
Look at the colours of my curving waves!
I am the effortless flowing river of creativity, indeed.

garche kab dekhte ho par dekho
aarzu hai k tum idhar dekho

You don't look at me,
but you should.

It is my ardent desire
that you should.

yuun araq jalva-gar hai us munh par
jis tarah os phuul par dekho

You have so much sweat
on your pretty face.
It looks like dewdrops
on a fresh flower.

dil hua hai taraf mohabbat ka
khuun ke qatre ka jigar dekho

Even the heart has become
a champion of love.
Look at the courage
of a drop of blood.

lutf mujh mein bhi hain hazaaron Mir
diidni huun jo soch kar dekho

I am filled with
countless delights, Mir.
I am worth a look
if you observe me
intently as you can.

Select Bibliography

Abdul Haq, Maulvi (*Baaba-e Urdu*). 2002. *Intikhaab-e Kalaam-e Mir*. New Delhi: Anjuman Taraqqi Urdu (Hind).

Abdullah, Syed. 1958. *Naqd-e Mir*. Lahore: Aaiina-e Adab.

Azad, Mohammad Husain. n.d. *Aab-e Hayaat*. Lahore: Malik Azad Book Depot.

Faruqi, Nisar Ahmed. 1994. *Mir Ki Aap Biti (Zikr-e Mir)*. New Delhi: Anjuman Taraqqi Urdu (Hind).

Faruqi, Nisar Ahmed. 2011. *Talash-e Mir*. New Delhi: Maktaba Jamia Ltd.

Hali, Altaf Hussain. 2013. *Muqaddama-e She'r o Shaa'yiri*. New Delhi: Maktaba Jamia.

Kazmi, Nasir. 2001. *Intikhaab-e Mir*. Lahore: Jahangir Book Depot.

Lakhnavi, Saa'dat Khan Nasir, Shamim Inhonavi, ed. 1971. *Tazkirah-e Khush Ma'rka Zeba*. Lucknow: Nasim Book Depot.

Lutf, Mirza Ali. Ata Kakovi ed. 1972. *Gulshan-e Hind*. Azeem Alshaan Book Depot.

Mir, Mir Taqi. 2007. *Kulliyaat-e Mir*. Vols. 1 & 2. New Delhi: National Council for Promotion of Urdu Language.

Mir, Mir Taqi. Mahmud Ilahi ed. 1984. *Tazkirah Nikat-us Sho'ra*. Lucknow: Uttar Pradesh Urdu Akademi.

Mir, Mir Taqi. Maulvi Abdul Haq ed. 1935 (1979 reprint). *Nikaat-us Sho'ra*. Karachi: Anjuman Taraqqi Urdu Pakistan.

Mus-hafi, Ghulam Hamdani. Maulvi Abdul Haq ed. 1933. *Tazkirah-e Hindi*. Delhi: Jaam'e Barqi Press.

Narang, Gopi Chand. 2013. *Usloobiyaat-e Meer*. Delhi: Educational Publishing House.

Narang, Gopi Chand. Surinder Deol trans. 2017. *Ghalib: Innovative Meanings and the Ingenious Mind*. New Delhi: Oxford University Press.

Narang, Gopi Chand. Surinder Deol trans. 2020. *The Urdu Ghazal: A Gift of India's Composite Culture*. New Delhi: Oxford University Press.

Shefta, Mustafa Khan. 1874. *Tazkirah Gulshan-e Be-khaar*. Lucknow: Nawal Kishore.